SpringerBriefs in Psychology

Behavioral Criminology

Series editor

Vincent B. Van Hasselt, Fort Lauderdale, USA

More information about this series at http://www.springer.com/series/10143

Nicole A. Sciarrino · Tyler Elizabeth Hernandez
Jennifer Davidtz

Understanding Child Neglect

Biopsychosocial Perspectives

Nicole A. Sciarrino
James A. Haley Veterans' Hospital
Tampa, FL, USA

Nova Southeastern University
Fort Lauderdale, FL, USA

Jennifer Davidtz
Nova Southeastern University
Fort Lauderdale, FL, USA

Tyler Elizabeth Hernandez
Nova Southeastern University
Fort Lauderdale, FL, USA

Henderson Behavioral Health
Hollywood, FL, USA

ISSN 2192-8363 ISSN 2192-8371 (electronic)
SpringerBriefs in Psychology
ISSN 2194-1866 ISSN 2194-1874 (electronic)
SpringerBriefs in Behavioral Criminology
ISBN 978-3-319-74810-8 ISBN 978-3-319-74811-5 (eBook)
https://doi.org/10.1007/978-3-319-74811-5

Library of Congress Control Number: 2018933455

© The Author(s) 2018

This work is subject to copyright. All rights are reserved by the Publisher, whether the whole or part of the material is concerned, specifically the rights of translation, reprinting, reuse of illustrations, recitation, broadcasting, reproduction on microfilms or in any other physical way, and transmission or information storage and retrieval, electronic adaptation, computer software, or by similar or dissimilar methodology now known or hereafter developed.

The use of general descriptive names, registered names, trademarks, service marks, etc. in this publication does not imply, even in the absence of a specific statement, that such names are exempt from the relevant protective laws and regulations and therefore free for general use.

The publisher, the authors and the editors are safe to assume that the advice and information in this book are believed to be true and accurate at the date of publication. Neither the publisher nor the authors or the editors give a warranty, express or implied, with respect to the material contained herein or for any errors or omissions that may have been made. The publisher remains neutral with regard to jurisdictional claims in published maps and institutional affiliations.

Printed on acid-free paper

This Springer imprint is published by the registered company Springer International Publishing AG part of Springer Nature.
The registered company address is: Gewerbestrasse 11, 6330 Cham, Switzerland

Contents

1 **Introduction**.. 1
  Defining Neglect... 2
  Clinical Conceptualization and Presentation 4
  Risk Factors Associated with Neglectful Parenting 7
  Child Risk Factors... 9
  Overview of Associated Consequences of Childhood Neglect........ 9

2 **The Effects of Childhood Neglect on Neurological Development**.... 11
  Overview of Neurodevelopment................................... 11
  Typical Development of Structures Most Impacted by Neglect..... 12
  Adverse Effects of Neglect on the Brain and Development........ 13
  Problems in Evaluating Adverse Neurological Changes Due to Neglect. 16
  How Are the Effects of Neglect on the Brain Mitigated?......... 17
  The Developing Brain and Assessment/Intervention 18

3 **Neglect and Attachment Insecurity**............................. 19
  Attachment Theory 19
  Neglect and Attachment Insecurity.............................. 21
  Neglect as it Relates to Romantic Relationships in Adulthood .. 23
  Summary.. 24

4 **The Sequelae of Neglect** 25
  Consequences of Neglect on Childhood
       and Adult Intellectual Functioning 26
  Impact of Neglect on Adult Psychopathology 27
  Interpersonal Problems and Impaired Emotion Regulation 30
  Outcomes on Physical Health.................................... 31
  The Impact of Neglect on Occupational Functioning and Offending.... 32
  Summary.. 33

5 **Assessment, Prevention, and Treatment** 35
  Assessment 35
  Primary and Secondary Prevention............................... 37
  Assessing the Effectiveness of Prevention Programs 39

    Reporting Neglect... 41
    Treatment Interventions for Families Characterized by Neglect 41
    Treatment for Adult Survivors of Neglect 42
    Conclusions.. 44

6 Clinical Case Examples 45
    Undetected Childhood Neglect................................. 45
    Childhood Neglect as a Precursor to Subsequent Abuse 46
    Childhood Neglect and Attachment Insecurity.................... 48

7 Unveiling Covert Abuse 51
    Future Directions 52

References 53

Chapter 1
Introduction

Differing forms of childhood maltreatment often co-occur (Allin, Wathen, & MacMillan, 2005; Glaser, 2000; Ney, Fung, & Wickett, 1994). However, when considering childhood physical abuse, sexual abuse, psychological abuse, and neglect, the latter has been identified as the type of childhood maltreatment with the greatest prevalence rate in several countries (Allin et al., 2005; Grassi-Oliveira & Stein, 2008; Hobbs & Wynne, 2002; U.S. Department of Health and Human Services, 2013). For instance, 78.3% of identified children who were subjects of child protective services reports in the United States were victims of neglect when compared to other maltreatment types (U.S. Department of Health and Human Services, 2013). Similarly, in one incidence report in Canada, neglect was the cause for child protective services reports in 40% of identified children (Allin et al., 2005). Neglect has also been suggested as a precursor to subsequent abuse (Gold, 2000; Ney et al., 1994). Regardless, despite the high frequency of its occurrence as compared with alternative forms of childhood maltreatment, there is a dearth of literature examining childhood neglect and its independent sequelae (De Bellis, 2005).

One explanation for the scarcity of research on this phenomenon may include difficulties operationalizing neglect (Caldwell, Bogat, & Davidson, 1988; Hobbs & Wynne, 2002). This may include the use of a more general definition of neglect or consideration of different subtypes (Allin et al., 2005). Additionally, a failure to discern between neglect and other types of abuse (e.g., physical, psychological, and sexual abuse) in the empirical literature may also pose a problem when exploring the implications of neglect on subsequent development. For example, various forms of child maltreatment are often examined jointly (e.g., physical abuse and neglect) due to difficulty establishing a sample where neglect is the only type of child maltreatment present (Allin et al., 2005; Caldwell et al., 1988; Hartley, 2002). Lastly, it has been proposed that there is less research on childhood neglect when compared to other types of childhood abuse due to the relationship between neglect and poverty, which may speak to the low social priority to reduce difficulties related to poverty (Dubowitz, 1994).

Defining Neglect

It can be difficult to distinguish between neglect and abuse; however, this delineation is important. Within the literature, it seems a universal understanding that abuse is characterized by an act done to a child, regardless of intent and physical or psychological consequences, whereas researchers propose that neglect is related to an absence of appropriate stimulation by the caregiver, resulting in a failure to meet the needs of a child (Straus, Kinard, & Williams, 1995; Teicher et al., 2004). This suggests that one primary difference between neglect and abuse is that neglect is associated more broadly with the relationship between the caregiver and child, whereas abuse refers to a specific event (Glaser, 2000).

There are practical and conceptual challenges to finding a consensus regarding how "neglect" should be defined (e.g., Allin et al., 2005; Caldwell et al., 1988; Moxley, Squires, & Lindstrom, 2012; Straus & Kantor, 2005). Efforts to reconcile several definitions of neglect denote neglect as a process (Tanner & Turney, 2003) in which there is failure of the caregiver to meet the developmental needs of the child, such as providing shelter, food, and affection, which change in form and intensity as the child ages (De Bellis, 2005; Straus & Kantor, 2005), as prescribed by the culture in which the child resides (Straus & Kantor, 2005). In other words, neglect is an "act of omission" (Allin et al., 2005, p. 498) that occurs when a child does not receive the fulfillment of a fundamental need that should be inherent within the family of origin in a given social context. For instance, in some cultures it may be socially acceptable to leave young children under the supervision of slightly older minor siblings, whereas in other cultures, this could be seen as a form of neglectful behavior by the caregiver in regards to supervision (Straus & Kantor, 2005). Moreover, determining neglectful behavior by a caregiver takes into account responsibilities of the caregiver. That is, in a home where there are two caregivers, a division of caregiver duties may render one caretaker neglectful and the other not, should one fail to follow through on his or her predetermined responsibilities to the child, such as providing food or picking the child up from school (Straus & Kantor, 2005).

Within the literature, several different classification systems of varying dimensions or subtypes of neglect have been established (e.g., Allin et al., 2005; Cowen, 1999; Straus et al., 1995). These categorizations include physical, emotional, medical, educational, nutritional, psychological, and environmental neglect; however, not all of these subtypes are present within each utilized classification system. Table 1.1 presents an overview of neglectful behavior, its various subtypes, and their definitions. For example, Straus et al. (1995) established a classification system, in which neglect was subdivided into four different categories for the purposes of

Table 1.1 Definitions of neglect subtypes

Subtype	Description
Neglect (General)	"Behavior by a caregiver that constitutes a failure to act in ways that are presumed by the culture of a society to be necessary to meet the developmental needs of a child and which are the responsibility of a caregiver to provide" (Straus & Kantor, 2005 p. 20). An act of omission resulting in the developmental needs of a child not being met (Allin et al., 2005). A failure to meet the basic needs of a child (e.g., shelter, nutrition, supervision, education, affection, and protection) when "financially able to do so or when offered reasonable means to do so" (Cowen, 1999 p. 401). Deprivation of necessities results in impairments in physical, mental, or emotional health, which excludes religious beliefs that do not allow for certain medical treatments (Florida Abuse Hotline, 2013).
Physical neglect	A failure to meet the physical needs of a child (Hildyard & Wolfe, 2002). "Harm or endangerment as a result of inadequate nutrition, clothing, hygiene, and supervision" (Kaplan, Pelcovitz, & Labruna, 1999 p. 1215). Failure to provide food, clothing, shelter, or medical care (Straus et al., 1995). Failure to provide housing that is appropriate, and failure to maintain clean clothing and appropriate hygiene (Cowen, 1999).
Emotional neglect	Acts of omissions by the caregiver often resulting in behavioral, cognitive, emotional, or mental illness (Hildyard & Wolfe, 2002). "Failure to provide adequate affection and emotional support or permitting a child to be exposed to domestic violence" (Kaplan et al., 1999 p. 1215). Lack of companionship, support, or affection (Straus et al., 1995).
Supervision neglect	Failure to set limits or attend to misbehaviors of the child, not being aware of a child's whereabouts (Straus et al., 1995). "Failure to provide attendance, guidance, and protection to children who, lacking experience and knowledge, cannot comprehend or anticipate dangerous situations" (Cowen, 1999 p. 402).
Cognitive neglect	Failure to assist a child with homework, or read to or play with the child (Straus et al., 1995).
Educational neglect	Failure to assure that a child consistently attends school or an equivalent at home study program (Cowen, 1999).
Nutritional neglect	Failure to appropriately provide food and fluids to a child in a way that is age appropriate and can result in a failure to thrive or dehydration (Cowen, 1999).
Health care/medical neglect	Failure to attend to a child when ill, failure to take appropriate preventative measures to keep a child from becoming sick, or failure to adhere to a doctor's recommendations (Cowen, 1999). Failure to provide appropriate healthcare (U.S. Department of Health and Human Services, 2013).
Abandonment	"Desertion of children on a permanent or temporary basis" (e.g., failure to retrieve a child from the babysitter) (Cowen, 1999 p. 402). Failure of the parent or caregiver to maintain or failure to establish a relationship (e.g., frequent or regular contact), or both (Florida Abuse Hotline, 2013).

developing a self-report measure of childhood neglect. This assessment includes emotional (e.g., lack of affection, companionship, or support), physical (e.g., lack of sufficient food, clothing, medical care), cognitive (e.g., not being played with or read to, or receiving assistance with schoolwork), and supervision (e.g., limit setting, attending to misbehavior) neglect (Straus et al., 1995). Based on conceptualization of the aforementioned subtypes, this classification subsumes educational neglect, and medical and nutritional neglect, within the cognitive and physical neglect dimensions, respectively. In contrast, the U.S. Department of Health and Human Services assesses for and identifies neglect as a general category, only delineating medical neglect and other child maltreatment (2013). Such a categorization lacks comprehensiveness and compounds the difficulty in assessing the associated consequences of ineffective, and insufficient parenting behaviors. Importantly, the incidence of various subtypes of neglect may be associated with independent risk factors and specific approaches to treatment, denoting the necessity for evaluating the *type* of neglect, rather than the presence of neglect more generally (Allin et al., 2005). Little information exists as to the similarities and differences of how different subtypes of neglect are caused, or the specific consequences associated with each subtype (Straus & Kantor, 2005).

In the federal legislation, the definition of neglect varies by state and is considered together with other forms of maltreatment (i.e., physical, sexual, and psychological abuse) under the Child Abuse Prevention and Treatment Act (CAPTA; Moxley et al., 2012; U.S. Department of Health and Human Services, 2013). The 2010 CAPTA amendment posits that child abuse and neglect involve the caregiver's act or failure to act in a situation that results in death, or presents an imminent risk of serious physical, emotional, or sexual harm or exploitation to a child (U.S. Department of Health and Human Services, 2013). In order to substantiate or confirm an allegation of child maltreatment, child protection laws often require the establishment of a pattern of abuse. Due to this requirement, individuals responsible for assessing or reporting neglect may develop "an implicit cultural tolerance for rarely occurring neglectful behavior by a caregiver" (Straus & Kantor, 2005 p. 24). This phenomenon may contribute to neglect being underreported and unrecognized.

Clinical Conceptualization and Presentation

Although, to the layperson, the word "neglect" is pejorative, our search of the literature revealed no research explicitly identifying neglect as purposeful or malevolent. In fact, it has been suggested that, when measuring neglectful behavior, the failure to meet the needs of a child should be considered neglectful, regardless of other circumstances or intent (Straus & Kantor, 2005). Consequently, it may be important to consider neglect as a passive, rather than active, process. For example, the Contextual Trauma Model (Gold, 2000) suggests that child abuse and maltreatment often occur in the context of a deficient family of origin that contributes to psychological difficulties and problems in adjustment by failing to provide adequate developmental resources for effective adult functioning. Viewing neglect as unintentional might assume that the parents in these families are lacking in skills and resources themselves, and therefore unable to transmit daily-living skills to their children, or provide a stable and supportive environment.

In applying neglect to the Contextual Trauma Model for conceptualization of subsequent difficulties (Gold, 2000), three levels of analysis are considered. The first involves assessing and treating the child or adult survivor's presenting problems, followed by remediating the deficits within the family context, and, finally, examining and understanding the role that society has played in supporting these deficits or inhibiting the development of more adaptive skills (Gold, 2000). Therefore, it may be insufficient to identify the presence of neglectful behavior by a caregiver and refer to Child Protective Services; rather, treatment should be encouraged for the child and family alike, as well as providing referrals to additional services within the community. In line with this conceptualization, neglect occurs within a system, involving the child's own characteristics coupled with family functioning and other environmental influences and risk factors, all contributing to the child's later development and adult functioning (Caldwell et al., 1988; Glaser, 2000; Moxley et al., 2012; Tanner & Turney, 2003). As a result, neglect has been traditionally understood according to Bronfenbrenner's Ecological Model (1979), which assesses various interacting systems, and the risk and protective factors that contribute to parenting behaviors and the child's welfare (e.g., Evans, Garner, & Honig, 2014; Moxley et al., 2012). Specifically, Bronfenbrenner's Ecological Model (1979) posits that the developing infant is shaped by the context into which it was born, and growth is dependent on the interplay between the multiple systems (e.g., microsystem, mesosystem, exosystem, macrosystem, chronosystem) that make up the child's environment. The microsystem is the most immediate to the growing individual and consists of the caregivers and siblings, school, peers, and work. These objects foster the child's development whether it be interpersonally, cognitively, or physically by interaction with the developing child. Mesosystems consist of the interplay between the developing child and two or more of these microsystems; for example, teachers and parents encouraging the child to take interest in school or the relationship between the family and the child's peer group. Exosystems, on the other hand, are composed of external factors that indirectly effect the developing child, such as the parent's workplace, extended family, mass media, and/or neighborhoods. The culture, laws, economic system, history, and customs into which the child is born comprise the macrosystem. Finally, the chronosystem relates to the time in which the child was born, specifically changes over time (Bronfenbrenner, 1979). Through this lens, we can see how neglect can result from parents lacking adequate social support, inflexible employment, or lack of parenting skills due to their own upbringing such that the parent may work long hours to provide for the child, but may miss opportunities to read, play, or interact with the child.

Neglectful behavior may not always produce direct harm to the child; and a child may not recognize the absence of certain parenting behaviors as being neglectful (e.g., not receiving a consequence for misbehaving, not being read to); however, the less frequently effective and attentive parenting occurs, the greater the risk to the child for developing adverse consequences (Straus & Kantor, 2005). This point underscores that it makes the most sense to define neglect by its adverse impact on the child's development, regardless of the caretakers' intent, the surrounding circumstances, or whether or not the child feels neglected. Additionally, lack of visible harm may contribute to difficulties in detecting the presence of neglect. In children, this may be further complicated when inquiring about caregiver behaviors that are deemed legally neglectful, as the child's experience of the behavior may be incongruous (Straus & Kantor, 2005). For example, a young child who can play independently may enjoy the freedom of being left home alone, and be unaware of the risks. This child may be unlikely to spontaneously report this neglect in the context of an open-ended inquiry. Moreover, although children may interpret neglect as traumatic (De Bellis, 2005; De Bellis, Hooper, Spratt, & Woolley, 2009) and as psychological abandonment by the parent (Gauthier, Stollak, Messé, & Aronoff, 1996), this is not necessarily the case for all children. As a result, a child reared in a home characterized by an absence of care can present with varying clinical presentations, depending upon whether or not the child perceives the caregiver's neglectful behavior as maltreatment.

Professionals with insufficient training may overlook signs of neglect; however, clinicians can be trained to attend to various clinical features that neglected children often exhibit (Hobbs & Wynne, 2002; Moxley et al., 2012). For example, children raised in neglectful homes may present with relational difficulties, including ruptures in attachment (Hobbs & Wynne, 2002; Moxley et al., 2012), impairments in social competence (Moxley et al., 2012; Tanner & Turney, 2003), and a sense of a lack of emotional nurturance (Hobbs & Wynne, 2002). These children may also exhibit delayed cognitive development (De Bellis, 2005; Moxley et al., 2012; Tanner & Turney, 2003), aggressiveness, truancy (Hobbs & Wynne, 2002), and behavioral problems (De Bellis, 2005; Glaser, 2000; Hobbs & Wynne, 2002). Furthermore, children reared in an ineffective family environment often have a history of sexual abuse (Gold, 2000; Hobbs & Wynne, 2002). Additionally, physical signs and symptoms of neglect can include poor hygiene, inappropriate clothing, physical injury (Hobbs & Wynne, 2002), and not meeting age appropriate height or weight goals (Moxley et al., 2012). The presence of these signs may suggest that a further assessment is warranted.

Taken together, children reared in an environment in which their developmental physical, emotional, supervision, and cognitive needs are not consistently met present with various difficulties. These difficulties can be more or less severe, depending upon the type, onset, chronicity, and severity of neglect (De Bellis, 2005; Glaser, 2000; Straus & Kantor, 2005). Problems in detection can compound these sequelae, as children often incur barriers to receiving appropriate intervention (Moxley et al., 2012). In adulthood, a history of childhood neglect is associated with a range of health problems, such as diabetes, obesity, substance use, heart disease, and autoimmune deficiencies (Moxley et al., 2012). (See Chap. 6 for several clinical illustrations of clients presenting in an outpatient setting for treatment associated with childhood neglect and abuse.)

Risk Factors Associated with Neglectful Parenting

Reviews of the literature of childhood neglect have identified family, as well as community and societal risk factors (e.g., Caldwell et al., 1988; Evans et al., 2014; Moxley et al., 2012). Risk factors commonly implicated in neglect include, but are not limited to, substance abuse (Barth, 2009; Evans et al., 2014), domestic violence and single-parent households (Evans et al., 2014; Hartley, 2002; Moxley et al., 2012), poverty (Caldwell et al., 1988; Evans et al., 2014; Moxley et al., 2012; Slack, Holl, McDaniel, Yoo, & Bolger, 2004), young maternal age, parental mental or physical illness, separation from mother for more than 3 months, unwanted pregnancy, and child characteristics (e.g., difficult temperament, behavioral problems) (Brown, Cohen, Johnson, & Salzinger, 1998).

Barth (2009) found that participants with a substance use problem were 4.2 times as likely to have neglected their children when compared to participants without substance use behaviors. The increased likelihood of neglectful parenting behaviors may be associated with a prioritization of substance use over other investments, resulting in failure to adequately meet the physical needs of the child (Barth, 2009). Parental substance use has been linked to a lack of parental monitoring due to preoccupation with substance abuse, lack of empathy toward the child, and expecting more from the child than is developmentally appropriate, for example feeding one's self or caring for siblings (Wells, 2006). Additionally, neglect has been associated with a sense of hopelessness within the family (Tanner & Turney, 2003). These risk factors provide support for a conceptualization of neglect through a contextual lens.

Low maternal age and education puts a child at risk for multiple types of child maltreatment including neglect (Brown et al., 1998). One can speculate that, because of the lack of education and life experience, these mothers are less equipped with understanding of child development, appropriate parenting practices, and may prioritize their own social life or interests over the child. For instance, it can be postulated that parents implicated in neglect exhibit their own inadequacies in modeling effective coping or providing appropriate resources due to themselves having been raised in ineffective environments in which they were not provided with adequate supervision (Gold, 2000; Strathearn, Gray, O'Callaghan, & Wood, 2001). Thus, the cycle of ineffective parenting and neglect continues into the next generation.

Poverty has been strongly associated with increased physical child neglect (Sedlak & Broadhurst, 1996; Slack et al., 2004). Various reasons are thought to explain the stark prevalence of child maltreatment in impoverished families, specifically perceived economic and material hardships, lack of employment or inconsistent employment, parental stress, and lack of social support or childcare (Slack et al., 2004). In addition to economic disadvantages, impoverished families often have parenting characteristics that are associated with child neglect, namely lack of warmth or physical affection, lack of knowledge in regards to typical child development, and utilization of spanking to discipline. Slack et al. (2004) found that higher levels of parental stress and perceived hardship were positively associated with more hostile and neglectful parenting practices and increased reports to Child Protective Services (CPS).

The relationship between poverty and neglect has been well established and has implications for the physical development of the child raised in a deficient environment (Caldwell et al., 1988; Hobbs & Wynne, 2002; Moxley et al., 2012). It is this association between poverty and neglect that has been proposed to contribute to the limited research examining this phenomenon (Hobbs & Wynne, 2002). This assumption may be due to a misconception that aspirations to enhance the environments of low socioeconomic status (SES) families are a fruitless endeavor. For example, malnutrition, also associated with poverty and nutritional neglect, can result in nonorganic failure to thrive, a retardation of the child's growth process (Hobbs & Wynne, 2002). Although impoverished families may encounter more difficulties providing material necessities to their children (Hobbs & Wynne, 2002), not all of these families fail to meet the developmental needs of their children, and families of a lower SES are certainly capable of providing adequate care for their children (Straus & Kantor, 2005). Nevertheless, our understanding of the degree to which low SES represents a risk factor for neglect suggests that resources devoted to enhancing the environments of low SES families may also serve to protect against neglect.

Another important risk factor for child neglect is maternal mental illness, whether it be anxiety, depression, or difficulties regulating emotions. For instance, maternal depression can be detrimental to mother-infant interactions and attachment styles; and mothers with depression may attend to their infants' needs inconsistently, may be hostile, and may avert their gaze from their infants (Boyd, Zayas, & McKee, 2006; Grace, Evindar, & Stewart, 2003). Mothers with peripartum depression (PPD) report difficulty enjoying, or disinterest in, the baby. They take a less active role with their babies. They often report an inability, or lack of attempts to, soothe the baby and, in some cases, mothers with PPD refuse to look at or hold their babies. Overall, there is a lack of synchronicity and reciprocity between mother and baby; that is, withdrawn mothers are less likely to respond to their infants' needs and, when they do, they lack affect. As a result, infants of withdrawn mothers develop passivity and withdraw from the mother as they learn they must self-regulate in order to regulate their emotions (Chaudron, 2003; Hart, Field, del Valle, & Pelaez-Nogueras, 1998). Changes in mother-infant interactions associated with PPD ultimately impact infants' developmental outcomes. Infants may exhibit developmental delays such as language deficits, social impairment, and cognitive delays (Boyd et al., 2006; Haga et al., 2012). In one study, infants whose mothers were depressed showed less emotional reciprocity, less interaction with others, and increased negative responses during interactions with others than infants whose mothers were not depressed (Stein et al., 1991). With increased avoidance behaviors, mothers suffering from depression are less likely to seek out their infants' attention and stimulate them through play or talking (Murray, 1992). Therefore, language skills and motor skills of infants whose mothers are depressed are often delayed (Boyd et al., 2006). These internalizing, externalizing, and developmental delays may have long lasting consequences, although research results about the effects of PPD on developmental outcomes in early childhood are inconsistent (Murray & Cooper, 1996). In other words, this is not to say that all mother who experience PPD are neglectful, only that PPD and other mental illnesses, when untreated and without social support, can result in neglectful parenting practices.

Child Risk Factors

The U.S. Department of Health and Human Services (2013) considers any child presenting with an intellectual disability, learning disability, emotional disturbance or behavioral problem, or physical/medical problem or impairment to be at an increased risk for childhood maltreatment (Brown et al., 1998). Due to the increased need for care in children presenting with a disability, parents presenting with their own unique risks may be unequipped to effectively care or provide for such children. Increased parental stress resulting from the demands of caring for a child with a physical or mental disability may explain increased child maltreatment in that increased parental stress is associated with hostile parenting practices (Slack et al., 2004).

Overview of Associated Consequences of Childhood Neglect

As stated above, there are multiple dimensions of neglect; however, there are limited data examining the risk factors and unique impact of each subtype on later functioning and adjustment (Allin et al., 2005; Straus & Kantor, 2005), as well as limited research on the impact of neglect, alone (Allin et al., 2005; Caldwell et al., 1988; Hartley, 2002). For example, in samples of childhood sexual abuse (CSA) survivors, empirical studies have identified neglect as having a negative impact on neurological functioning (Bogdan, Williamson, & Hariri, 2012; Glaser, 2000) and attachment formation (Bifulco et al., 2006; Glaser, 2000). In assessing the "worst" combinations of childhood abuse and neglect in children, physical neglect, physical abuse, and verbal abuse had the greatest negative impact on enjoyment of living and hopes for the future (Ney et al., 1994). Moreover, in studies independently examining the effects of neglect and physical abuse on psychological functioning, childhood neglect was associated with more severe psychopathology and interpersonal problems in young adulthood, when compared to survivors of physical abuse, alone (Gauthier et al., 1996). Gauthier et al. (1996) suggest that this may be due to perceived abandonment associated with a lack of care (i.e., neglect). Consequently, it is evident that neglect, separate from other forms of child maltreatment, is associated with adverse outcomes in adulthood and requires further investigation.

Due to the prevalence of childhood neglect in the U.S., it is imperative to identify family and contextual risk factors, as well as the early signs and symptoms of neglect in children. Neglectful and ineffective parenting has been demonstrated to increase risk for a multitude of difficulties, including impairments in neurological and cognitive functioning, attachment security, and psychopathology. Although some of the problematic consequences of neglect are evident in early childhood, other difficulties may manifest later in adolescence or adulthood. This reference on childhood neglect highlights the difficulties in effectively defining and assessing for neglectful behavior. Moreover, it explores the research examining the impact of the various subtypes of neglect on child and adult functioning across several domains, and integrates additional research findings, which have evaluated neglect within the context of other forms of child maltreatment.

Chapter 2
The Effects of Childhood Neglect on Neurological Development

Brain maturation occurs continuously from birth into young adulthood (Carlson, 2013; De Bellis, 2005) with continued modifications throughout life associated with exposure to sensory stimulation and experience (Carlson, 2013; Perry, 2002; Joseph, 1999). However, the early childhood environment plays an integral role in the neurodevelopmental process (Perry, 2002), such that a lack of sensory stimulation and experience (e.g., physical and cognitive neglect) can contribute to adverse neurological functioning. Consequently, altered neurological development associated with an impoverished childhood environment can present in childhood and remain into adulthood (De Bellis, 2005; Glaser, 2000; Joseph, 1999; Perry, 2002).

Overview of Neurodevelopment

In typical neurodevelopment, the first stage, neurogenesis, occurs in utero during the second and third trimesters and involves the birth of neurons via stem cells known as progenitor cells (Carlson, 2013; Perry, 2002). These cells begin to divide and give rise to the central nervous system, that is, the brain and spinal cord (Carlson, 2013). Although humans possess the majority of lifetime neurons at birth, stimulation from the environment and experience facilitate the establishment of connections between neurons and foster brain development and growth (Carlson, 2013; Perry, 2002).

A combination of genetic predispositions and environmental experiences significantly impact the subsequent migration and differentiation processes of cells. In addition, a lack of environmental input in postnatal development alters the expression of certain genes and can negatively impact the developmental process (Perry, 2002). During migration and differentiation, neurons arrive at various locations in the brain and assume a specialization in function within a particular brain region (e.g., visual processing, motor control) (Carlson, 2013; Perry, 2002). Repetitive stimulation and experience facilitate the neurons in forming connections to communicate and transmit messages with one another. In other words, sensory input in postnatal brain development affects the connections established between neurons, the speed at which they communicate with one another, and the death of neurons that are less frequently activated (Carlson, 2013; Perry, 2002). For example, during the more experience-sensitive phases of neuronal development, recurring experiences serve to strengthen the formation of various connections, increasing the speed at which the neurons communicate through a thickening of myelin sheath covering the axon of the neuron—the part of the cell responsible for transmitting messages from the cell body to the presynaptic release point (i.e., terminal buttons) (Carlson, 2013; Perry, 2002). Taken together, these cellular processes contribute to the formation of larger structures that are involved in daily functioning. Similarly, in animals raised in an enriched environment, research has noted the development of a larger, more complex brain, and greater flexibility in brain functioning when compared to animals raised in a more deficient environment (e.g., under deprivation conditions) (Perry, 2002).

The brain develops sequentially, yielding different critical periods of development for various neurological structures. Research examining neglect and the brain has found that impairment of some specific structures may have more adverse consequences than impairment of others. These areas include the structures of the limbic system (e.g., amygdala, hippocampus, and septal nuclei), corpus callosum, and prefrontal cortex (Bogdan, Williamson, & Hariri, 2012; Carlson, 2013; De Bellis, 2005; Glaser, 2000; Joseph, 1999; Maheu et al., 2010; Teicher et al., 2004).

Typical Development of Structures Most Impacted by Neglect

The progenitor cells described above give rise to each of the layers that comprise the two hemispheres of the cerebral cortex. The cerebral cortex is characterized by bulges and grooves, referred to as gyri and sulci, which serve to increase the surface area of the brain. This area contains the primary visual, auditory, motor, and somatosensory cortices, and the neuronal connections that extend into the deeper layers of the brain are strengthened through postnatal experiences (Carlson, 2013). While the brain is subdivided into many regions, one of the more important and evolutionarily new areas of the brain, the prefrontal cortex, is heavily involved in learning, memory, planning, and problem solving (Carlson, 2013).

The two hemispheres of the cerebral cortex are joined by a band of fibers known as the corpus callosum, which facilitates communication between the two hemispheres (Carlson, 2013). In contrast to the slower development of the limbic system, the fibers of the corpus callosum are present at birth (Carlson, 2013). Although differences in shape can present in typically developing males and females (Carlson, 2013), experience has been found to contribute to a decrease in size in young adulthood when neglect is present in early childhood (Teicher et al., 2004). In one study, the reduction in size of the corpus callosum was especially marked in males, suggesting that neglect had a greater impact in boys than in girls, and compared to other types of abuse (Teicher et al., 2004).

The limbic system is housed within the temporal lobe of the cerebral cortex and is comprised of several structures, which collectively are responsible for motivation, learning and memory, emotion, and monitoring hunger and thirst (Carlson, 2013; Joseph, 1999). These structures develop in response to the presence of interpersonal, physical, and cognitive stimuli and do so at different rates, with the amygdala developing much more rapidly within the first year of life and the septal nuclei maturing later in childhood (Joseph, 1999). In young children, the underdeveloped limbic system structures are responsible for engaging in behaviors that yield physical contact and attention from others to foster growth and survival, such that within the first year of life, children will respond indiscriminately to attention from others in an effort to have their fundamental needs for attention and physical touch met (Joseph, 1999). However, with appropriate social contact and stimulation, the maturation of the amygdala fosters feelings of wariness of strangers and provides the ability to establish more selective relationships (Joseph, 1999). As a result, children become more cautious as they get older and form attachments to individuals who are more consistently available.

Adverse Effects of Neglect on the Brain and Development

Neurodevelopment has been described as a continuous, "activity-dependent" process with critical periods associated with the development of specific brain regions (Perry, 2002). The sequential nature of neurodevelopment begins with areas of least complexity to those of most complexity, rendering certain brain regions more vulnerable to the negative effects of a lack of stimulation at differing times (Carlson, 2013; Perry, 2002). In other words, the developmental needs of the child change from year to year and a lack of stimulation during specific windows of vulnerability can produce a delay in, or complete absence of, certain skills acquisition (Glaser, 2000).

Although the existing research examining the implications of neglect on neurodevelopment has focused more generally on neglect, it is reasonable to draw conclusions such that specific subtypes of neglect may present unique adverse effects to development. For instance, physical touch is imperative for survival in infants (Joseph, 1999); as a result, severe emotional neglect in early childhood, in which the child is not being provided with sufficient caregiver contact and affection, can result in death, whereas the absence of these interactions in late adolescence may have much less severe consequences. This may imply that the subtype of neglect could have varying developmental consequences depending upon the child's age. Therefore, the age of onset, nature, and duration of neglect has implications in neurodevelopment (De Bellis, 2005). In addition, if a child is reared in an environment where severe medical neglect is present and the child requires glasses to correct visual problems, but never receives the appropriate medical care, the neurons in the brain responsible for visual stimulation will not be appropriately stimulated, possibly resulting in perceptual blindness and long-term visual impairment due to a decrease in the presence of visual input to the brain (Joseph, 1999). Similarly, severe medical neglect for infants with ear infections that cause hearing problems, can result in difficulties learning new information and can also undermine speech and language acquisition.

For many children, neglect is perceived as a stressful experience (Glaser, 2000; Moxley, Squires, & Lindstrom, 2012). Although it has long been understood that stress within the family is a risk factor for neglectful caregiving behaviors (Caldwell, Bogat, & Davidson, 1988), stress for the developing child has been identified as a risk factor for impairments across developmental domains (Carlson, 2013; Glaser, 2000; Moxley et al., 2012; Perry, 2002). In an impoverished environment, the limbic system develops abnormalities, which impair the child's ability to identify, process, and respond to social and emotional stimuli (Joseph, 1999). These impairments can result in indiscriminate attachment relationships, aggressive outbursts, obsessive and repetitive behaviors, and impairments in learning and memory, among other sequelae (Joseph, 1999). For example, one study examining the impact of low childhood SES—a situation associated with stress—and child maltreatment on hippocampal and amygdala volume in a sample of adults revealed decreased hippocampal volume in those reporting a history of childhood maltreatment (i.e., neglect, abuse, exposure to domestic violence) (Lawson et al., 2017). The authors postulate that the stress of childhood maltreatment and poverty effect the brain differently possibly due to the characteristics of the abuse (e.g., duration, intensity) and impact of neglect on attachment formation and cognitive functioning (Lawson et al., 2017). In addition to hippocampal volume, exposure to stress can negatively impact neuronal development in the hippocampus, an area of the brain associated with learning and memory, and may result in hippocampal atrophy (Carlson, 2013; Joseph, 1999). That is, stress associated with neglect in early life activates the hypothalamic-pituitary-adrenal (HPA) axis, sympathetic nervous system, neurotransmitter system, and immune system (De Bellis, 2005; Glaser, 2000). Alterations in activation of the HPA axis inhibit the production of the stress hormone cortisol, which has been associated with becoming desensitized to stressful situations in those with chronic abuse and neglect in childhood (Glaser, 2000), thereby decreasing the responsiveness of childhood abuse and maltreatment survivors when faced with subsequent, potentially dangerous, situations.

Neglect has also been found to contribute to deficits in amygdala functioning (Bogdan et al., 2012; Joseph, 1999; Maheu et al., 2010). The amygdala, one of the most crucial parts of the limbic system, is responsible for the recognition, feeling, and expression of emotional stimuli (Carlson, 2013; Joseph, 1999), as well as the development of attachment relationships (Joseph, 1999). Underdevelopment of the structures within the limbic system (e.g., amygdala, cingulate gyrus, septal nuclei) may prompt aberrant social and emotional behaviors, which can contribute to indiscriminate attention-seeking and obsessive and repetitive behaviors (Joseph, 1999). Previous research has linked caregiver deprivation and emotional neglect with sensitivity to threatening cues, which has revealed greater left amygdala and hippocampus activation when processing threatening stimuli (Maheu et al., 2010). Moreover, research utilizing blood-oxygen-level dependent (BOLD) fMRIs has found that emotional neglect can significantly predict elevations in threat-related amygdala reactivity, thus providing support for the existing literature that stress in childhood and early adolescence can have an adverse effect on the development of the amygdala, including structural enlargement (Bogdan et al., 2012). Further, and also associated with alterations in amygdala functioning, neglected children exhibit impairments in recognizing different facial expressions when compared to non-neglected controls (Maheu et al., 2010). Considered jointly with the abovementioned limbic system deficits, compromised emotional processing and memory impairments could be attributed, in part, to difficulties with facial expression recognition. Lastly, although outside of the scope of this chapter, it is important to consider how neurological changes associated with neglect impact later psychopathology. For example, children who have been abused or neglected manifest with neurological changes to the amygdala that may be associated with later psychopathology, such as PTSD. More specifically, the researchers found that greater emotional neglect was associated with elevated threat-related amygdala activity, which may be associated with stress-related disorders (Bogdan et al., 2012).

Regarding corpus callosum development, one study examining the impact of neglect, physical and sexual abuse, psychiatric illness, and gender, found that neglect significantly contributed to decreased corpus callosum volume when controlling for other variables (Teicher et al., 2004). This finding was especially apparent in males, which might suggest that males are especially vulnerable to the negative effects of a neglectful family of origin and that their development may be more markedly impacted by early interactions and experiences (De Bellis, 2005; Teicher et al., 2004). Decreased corpus callosum volume might impact the rate at which the right and left hemispheres communicate with one another or negatively impact awareness. In contrast, adverse effects to the prefrontal cortex are evident in persistent social, behavioral, and cognitive deficits (De Bellis, 2005). Learning difficulties and cognitive impairments are commonly observed in children reared in deficient environments (De Bellis, 2005; Maheu et al., 2010; Strathearn, Gray, O'Callaghan, & Wood, 2001). For example, Strathearn et al. (2001) found neglect to be the only type of maltreatment risk factor associated with cognitive delay and impairment in a sample of low weight infants. Additionally, the infants identified as having a history of neglect exhibited a decline in cognitive functioning from their first to second year of life (Strathearn et al., 2001). These results have been supported by recent research suggesting that children with a history of neglect are at an increased risk for learning disabilities (De Bellis, 2005; Moxley et al., 2012). However, children removed from neglectful environments and placed in more nurturing, enriching environments in early childhood have demonstrated the ability to recoup previously forfeited developmental processes (Perry, 2002). Additionally, a smaller head circumference was noted when comparing children with a history of neglect to those with no history of neglect or other forms of child abuse (e.g., physical abuse) (Strathearn et al., 2001). This finding has been validated in previous studies through the use of MRI and CT scans, when available (Perry, 2002).

In summary, without sufficient stimulation, various brain regions may be underdeveloped, atrophy, exhibit abnormal activity, form or maintain inappropriate or random interconnections, or come to be invaded by competing brain regions. This, in turn, may result in impairments in neuronal communication, learning, memory, emotion identification and processing, attachment, and interpersonal functioning (Carlson, 2013; Joseph, 1999; Perry, 2002). The aforementioned findings provide further evidence for the inherent need to effectively assess family environments with a potential for neglect and provide early intervention. Such actions can serve to mitigate the consequences of compromised neurological development, subsequently reducing the likelihood for cognitive impairments and other adverse outcomes.

Problems in Evaluating Adverse Neurological Changes Due to Neglect

Due to the frequency at which various types of child maltreatment co-occur, it is difficult to evaluate the impact of neglect alone on neurological development (De Bellis, 2005; Glaser, 2000). That is, identifying neglected children in the absence of other forms of child maltreatment is problematic from an empirical standpoint. As a result, much research examining the detrimental consequences of neglect on the brain has been conducted through animal studies (De Bellis, 2005). For instance, in animal studies of infant rats and monkeys, maternal deprivation has been found to result in impairments of social, behavioral, and cognitive developments. These deficiencies include, but are not limited to, impairments in attention, capacity for learning, and emotion regulation. Similarly, rhesus monkeys reared in insolation presented with autistic-like social deficits (De Bellis, 2005). These studies provide support for the existing literature involving children and adult survivors of childhood neglect, such that deprivation of care has neurological implications across several domains of functioning (e.g., Carlson, 2013; Glaser, 2000; Moxley et al., 2012; Perry, 2002). Additionally, research examining neglect in animals bolsters the need for continued assessment and intervention in children and adults with a history of childhood neglect due to the potential for the aforementioned functional impairments. However, although important to understand the independent sequelae of neglect, research examining adverse neurological development in survivors of both childhood maltreatment and neglect may be more generalizable due to the frequency at which neglect co-occurs with other forms of maltreatment.

How Are the Effects of Neglect on the Brain Mitigated?

Neuroplasticity in childhood can mitigate the effects of early childhood neglect, especially when coupled with early intervention (De Bellis, 2005). This speaks to the importance of early identification and treatment of children in deficient environments, such that appropriate interventions may mitigate the presence of later neurological deficits. For example, removing children from neglectful environments has been found to contribute to improvements in intellectual functioning (Perry, 2002). In addition, although it was initially believed that the production of new neurons could not occur after the brain had been fully developed, this notion has since been refuted (Carlson, 2013). The development of new neuronal connections in adulthood has clinical implications for children reared in neglectful environments, in that adult experiences may allow for improvements in neurological functioning.

Lower levels of neglect, characterized by some social contact by caregivers, may result in reasonably normal functioning (Joseph, 1999). For instance, in a study examining the adverse effects of neglect and physical abuse, results revealed that psychological functioning is more impaired in those with a history of neglect as compared to physical abuse (Gauthier, Stollak, Messé, & Aronoff, 1996). Consequently, these results provide additional support for more severe implications regarding a lack of parental care and contact as compared to parental contact that may be abusive in nature (i.e., physical abuse) (Gauthier et al., 1996). Similarly, this finding can be applied to the development of the limbic system, such that young children persistently seek attention and contact from their mothers, even when faced with physical violence (Joseph, 1999), thereby emphasizing the innate drive for parental support, regardless of the potential consequences. Additionally, research examining neurodevelopment in orphans and animals under deprivation conditions reveals that emotional attachments are imperative for appropriate development. Without these primary attachments, cognitive deficits often occur (Perry, 2002). Caregiver deprivation, which refers to children who have been separated from their primary caregivers and placed in orphanages or foster care, has been associated with emotional problems (Maheu et al., 2010). Research utilizing fMRI suggests that the resulting emotional difficulties might be associated with greater medial temporal lobe activation coupled with attachment insecurity (Maheu et al., 2010). Moreover, medial temporal lobe activation was significantly correlated with the number of foster home placements and negatively associated with time spent with an adoptive family (Maheu et al., 2010), thereby providing additional support for the probable role of attachment in mitigating the adverse impact of neglect on brain development in children with caregiver deprivation or emotional neglect.

The Developing Brain and Assessment/Intervention

As a result of changes in the developmental needs of the child, assessing for and identifying neglectful caregiver behavior may prove challenging. Given the changing demands of the child during development, various assessment protocols and procedures may be required to better evaluate neglect at different ages (Perry, 2002). Consequently, primary school teachers may be at an advantage for identifying children reared in neglectful environments, such that they may be more cognizant of typical intellectual functioning in school-age children and changes in academic progress. From a Contextual Trauma Model (Gold, 2000), detection and intervention by primary school teachers, whether it be a call to the child's parents or a referral to a child protective services agency, demonstrates effective intervening with the social context, thereby providing opportunities for change within the family system. Given that the literature suggests that the negative effects of neglect and maltreatment on the brain may be reversible if the child is removed from the environment and placed in a more enriching one, early detection continues to be of the utmost importance (Watts-English, Fortson, Gibler, Hooper, & De Bellis, 2006).

Chapter 3
Neglect and Attachment Insecurity

The parent-infant relationship serves as a blueprint for future relationships with others and the world. From this relationship, the infant learns whether he can depend on others to meet his needs, whether he can communicate with others effectively, and whether it is safe to explore his world. Attachment theory postulates that the parent-infant relationship provides the infant with the first opportunity to form a secure attachment to another human being, ideally characterized by warmth, trust, synchronicity, and reciprocity (Bowlby, 1969). However, in cases of childhood neglect, the parent or caregiver has not provided the scaffolding necessary for establishing a secure attachment. Consequently, neglect has been linked to increased psychological problems (e.g., depression and anxiety) and attachment insecurity in children and adolescents (Claussen & Crittenden, 1991; Gauthier, Stollak, Messé, & Aronoff, 1996; Hobbs & Wynne, 2002; Shipman, Edwards, Brown, Swisher, & Jennings, 2005). This chapter will include a brief discussion of attachment theory, attachment insecurity, and the impact of neglect on attachment. Additionally, implications for romantic relationships for individuals reared in a neglectful family of origin will be discussed.

Attachment Theory

Bowlby and Ainsworth's early attachment theory emphasized the need for young children to develop a secure dependence on their primary caretakers in order to explore unfamiliar situations while maintaining access to their caretakers for comfort and encouragement, as needed (Bretherton, 1992). As a result, secure attachment develops when caregivers are reliable and accessible, serving to reassure the child that they are available, especially during times of perceived danger or fear (Alexander, 2009). Furthermore, attachment theory posits that mutual interaction between the parent and the infant is critical to healthy development; i.e., both the parent and the child should be responsive to each other's affective displays (Bowlby,

1969; Bretherton, 1992; Erickson, Egeland, & Pianta, 1989, Stern, 1985). Stimulating and responsive interaction between the parent and infant fosters language development, emotion regulation, mentalization, and other facets of healthy development (Allen & Oliver, 1982; Borelli, Compare, Snavely, & Decio, 2015; Frodi & Smetana, 1984). For example, Borelli et al. (2015) posit that mentalization, i.e., the ability to understand that mental states influence one's behavior, is fostered through the caregiver's contingent mirroring of the infant's affect. When the caregiver is able to mirror frustration, pain, or joy back to the infant, the infant is better able to understand his own internal state (e.g., frustration, pain, joy) and becomes able to identify these internal states independently throughout development. However, this requires a sensitive and perceptive caregiver who is engaged in the infant's healthy development. Since mentalization is a developmentally acquired skill, the infant relies on the caregiver to identify his mental and affect states prior to mastering mentalization (Borelli et al., 2015).

It is the role of the caregiver of young infants to mediate the effect between environmental influences and subsequent development; the caregiver is expected to teach and model emotional and behavioral responses to novel experiences so that the infant can learn how to respond independently (Glaser, 2000; Kim & Cicchetti, 2010). Ainsworth's Strange Situation study (1970) identified three different attachment styles, secure attachment, avoidant attachment, and ambivalent/resistant attachment, when looking at infants' affective and behavioral reactions to being separated from, and then reunited with, their mothers. Secure attachment is the ideal attachment relationship between the mother and child; 70% of infants were securely attached to their mothers. Securely attached infants were distressed when their mothers left the room and were avoidant of the stranger in the room when their mother was not present; however, they were friendly to stranger when their mother was present, using her as a safe base to explore and play with others. When the securely attached infant was reunited with his mother, the infant was happy and easy to soothe. Bowlby proposed that these early relational patterns lead to the formation of internal working models of interpersonal relationship patterns, which subsequently shape the child's understanding of and interactions with others, the world, and the way in which they aim to have their attachment needs fulfilled (Collins & Allard, 2001). Accordingly, adults with positive memories and appraisals of their caregivers from early childhood develop internal working models that result in attachment security (Collins & Allard, 2001).

On the other hand, in Ainsworth's Strange Situation (1970), infants who were avoidantly attached (15% of infants) displayed no distress when the mother left, did not avoid or fear the stranger, played normally with or without the mother present, did not acknowledge the mother when she returned, and were equally soothed by both the mother and the stranger. This is in stark contrast to the behavior of the securely attached infants; and this attachment style is associated with caregivers that are insensitive and unavailable to the infant's emotional, physical, and psychological needs. An avoidantly attached infant's mother often responds inappropriately to the infant's needs or ignores them completely; thus, the infant withdraws from the mother, as he has learned that his mother will not fulfill his needs no matter how distressed he may appear (Ainsworth and Bell, 1970).

The third attachment style described by Ainsworth and Bell (1970) is the ambivalent/resistant attachment style, which is a result of inconsistent sensitivity to the infant's needs. The infant who is ambivalently attached is unsure whether or not the mother will respond this time and is resistant to her leaving or letting her soothe him upon her return. These infants demonstrated intense distress when their mothers left, but were also fearful and disengaged with the stranger. They explored less and cried more than securely and avoidantly attached infants. Interestingly, the ambivalently attached infants in the Strange Situation (Ainsworth and Bell, 1970) approached the mother upon return, but then resisted her comforting behaviors by taking longer to be soothed or pushing her away. While securely attached infants were the majority (70%) in Ainsworth's study (1970), it is arguably more important to understand the remaining 30% of infants who demonstrated insecure attachment styles because of the myriad negative psychological and developmental outcomes associated with insecure attachment, such as depression, anxiety, cognitive delays, language deficits, etc. (Boyd, Zayas, & McKee, 2006; Erickson et al., 1989; Gauthier et al., 1996; Spertus, Yehuda, Wong, Halligan, & Seremetis, 2003).

Neglect and Attachment Insecurity

One of the clinical features of neglect is a disruption in attachment capacity and relationships (Hobbs & Wynne, 2002). When caretakers exhibit inconsistencies in comforting or being readily available to their children, those children may display attachment insecurity in relation to their caretakers (Bretherton, 1992). Additionally, inconsistent environments and caregivers (e.g., different foster families) contribute to attachment insecurity. For instance, repeated moves of youths from one living environment to another are thought to enhance stress and to prevent the establishment of a secure attachment relationship with caregivers, leading to impaired development (Maheu et al., 2010). This may be because repeated moves make it nearly impossible for youths to form, maintain, and expect consistent reciprocal relationships with their caregivers within a single family/location let alone between locations as some caregivers may be responsive and others may not. A lack of physical and emotional connection to the parent, or an inconsistent connection, results in the child feeling disconnected from the parent, and unsure of how to respond to others in the environment.

Neglectful parents are less likely to teach their children the necessary emotion regulation skills needed to be able to identify and discriminate between emotions, modulate emotions, or practice perspective-taking (Kim & Cicchetti, 2010). In contrast to appropriately modeled emotion regulation skills in children reared in healthy families, children reared in neglectful or abusive families do not have their emotions mirrored back to them – in fact, the internal states of the children are often denied, invalidated (e.g., "You have no reason to be crying." "You are not hurt."), or completely ignored. The literature contends that lack of contact, physically and emotionally, can be severely detrimental to the psychological, emotional, and cognitive development of young children (Gauthier et al., 1996; Maheu et al., 2010). Infants whose mothers are distant and disengaged exhibit developmental delays such as language deficits, social impairment, and cognitive delays (Boyd et al., 2006; Haga et al., 2012). The lack of interaction, whether it be verbal, sensory, or emotional neglect, results in skills deficits that impact the child's ability to communicate effectively with others. Emotionally neglected infants show less emotional reciprocity, less interaction with others, and increased negative responses during interactions with others – that is, these infants cry more frequently, are more fussy, are resistant to being held, smile less and do not try to engage others. Additionally, emotionally neglected infants often exhibit apprehension towards their mother and others, appearing to be withdrawn and listless, both indications of attachment insecurity (Ainsworth & Wittig, 1969; Murray, 1992; Stein et al., 1991).

Research by Gauthier et al. (1996) established that children reared in the absence of parental involvement (i.e., neglect) experienced greater psychological problems and attachment difficulties when compared to children who experienced physical abuse. Similarly, longitudinal research conducted by Erickson et al. (1989) found that children ages two to six who were neglected and whose mothers were psychologically unavailable, when compared to children who were physically and verbally abused, had significantly greater intellectual and social deficits, including attachment insecurity. These results may suggest that physical abuse—although harmful and associated with negative outcomes—affords some form of physical contact and connectedness with the caregiver, whereas neglect does not. Dean, Malik, Richards, and Stringer (1986) postulated that neglected children interpret their parents' complete disengagement as rejection of them regardless of their behavior; the children perceive that they are unworthy of their parents' time, love, and attention. This sense of worthlessness is unique to neglected children when compared to physically abused children; physically abused children, according to Dean et al. (1986), interpret their parents' harsh punishment as a result of their misbehavior rather than who they are as a person. This rationalization of parental mistreatment seen in physically abused children serves as a buffer when considering later psychological problems, such as anxiety, depression, somatization, paranoia, and hostility. Consequently, the researchers postulated that neglect might be a better predictor of later mental health and interpersonal stressors (Gauthier et al., 1996). Clinical implications for these findings highlight the importance of attachment formation on later psychological and relational functioning due to the lack of interaction between the neglected child and caregiver. Additionally, the importance of early intervention is essential to mitigate these negative psychological, developmental, and relational outcomes.

Previous literature examining attachment formation has suggested that attachment style is continuously revised, albeit gradually and slowly throughout the lifetime (Levy, Ellison, Scott, & Bernecker, 2011). For instance, a study examining attachment in the adoption of children aged 4–7 years old found that, when placed in the homes of secure mothers, the insecurely attached late-placed children were successful in revising their attachment style and establishing attachment security

(Pace & Zavattini, 2011). In contrast, the matched control children who also presented with attachment insecurity did not exhibit a significant change in their attachment style (Pace & Zavattini, 2011). Although there is no specific critical period associated with attachment formation, internal working models become relatively stable in early childhood (Sroufe, 1988), which may be supported by the results of the aforementioned study, such that attachment may become relatively stable by age seven. These findings emphasize the importance of early intervention in providing corrective experiences and alternative attachment relationships to counter attachment insecurity and neglect within the family of origin.

Neglect as it Relates to Romantic Relationships in Adulthood

The literature contends that interparental relationships heavily influence relationship expectations for future romantic relationships, communication skills, conflict resolution styles, and perceived closeness to others (Crockett & Randall, 2006; Maleck & Papp, 2015; Roisman, Collins, Sroufe, & Egeland, 2005; Weigel, 2007). Parental relationships serve as models for children's future relationship expectations and for interpersonal behavioral patterns that they will enact in future relationships. For these reasons, it is particularly important when considering individuals who experienced childhood neglect, abuse, or interparental conflict as they may have witnessed poor interparental relationships marked by abuse, infidelity, lack of communication, and/or detachment. Children reared in at-risk family environments, defined as family environments marked by neglect, maltreatment, and high levels of conflict and/or aggression, exhibit negative romantic relationship outcomes (Maleck & Papp, 2015). In adulthood, attachment insecurity may manifest through discomfort associated with closeness and difficulties trusting others (i.e., avoidant), or through the perception of others as unwilling to establish close relationships and a resulting fear of abandonment (i.e., anxious/ambivalent) (Hazan & Shaver, 1987).

Research examining adult attachment style has been conducted in the context of childhood abuse more generally as abuse and neglect rarely occur in isolation. This is important to consider because the extant of the literature shows that the combination of abuse and neglect results in variable attachment styles and negative psychological outcomes. Adult attachment style has been implicated as a mediator between childhood neglect/abuse and adult experiences of depression and anxiety (Bifulco et al., 2006). Specifically, childhood neglect/abuse was significantly related to adult attachment insecurity, when accounting for the indirect effect of fearful and angry-dismissive attachment styles. Although in this study childhood neglect and abuse were combined as predictors, when jointly considered with the extant literature, it can be concluded that a history of childhood neglect adversely influences later functioning, when considering relational patterns.

Maleck and Papp (2015) examined couple's interactions during a staged conflict and found that males (but not females) who were reared in at-risk families did not use effective communication skills. These behaviors were rated by trained observers and were, therefore, unaffected by self-report bias. These gender differences might be explained by relational differences evident in male and female youths which foster different skills and opportunities for practicing different forms of communication. For instance, females engage in more self-disclosure and intimacy in their friendships, thereby allowing greater opportunities for remediating communication skills and replacing ineffective relational patterns modeled from their families of origin. Males' friendships, on the other hand, are characterized by shared activities and competition, resulting in fewer opportunities to foster new patterns of communication (Underwood & Rosen, 2009). Interestingly, there were no reliable associations when individuals reared in at-risk family environments were asked to rate their satisfaction with their current relationship (Maleck & Papp, 2015).

Summary

The effects of neglect permeate multiple facets of development, hindering social, emotional, physical, and attachment development throughout the lifespan. Children who were reared in neglectful families exhibit language deficits, interpersonal deficits, cognitive deficits, psychological issues, and attachment insecurity. Specifically, neglect can disrupt and impede the development of attachment security between an infant and his caregiver due to the lack of interaction between the caregiver and child, necessary modeling of appropriate emotion regulation skills, and trust that the caregiver will meet the infant's needs. Since the parent-child relationship provides the blueprint for future relationships, it is important to understand the influence of neglect on attachment in this fundamental relationship. Doing so might facilitate recognizing the symptoms sooner, intervening earlier, and treating attachment insecurity more effectively, thus increasing the likelihood that individuals reared in neglectful environments will have meaningful and mutually gratifying relationships.

Chapter 4
The Sequelae of Neglect

In childhood, abused and neglected individuals can develop seemingly functional coping strategies and behaviors; however, certain internalizing and externalizing behaviors can become increasingly maladaptive at subsequent developmental stages, contributing to the development of further difficulties (Widom, 2000). Although the impact of neglect is not as well understood as that of abuse, research examining individuals reporting perceived childhood neglect, as well as survivors of co-occurring childhood maltreatment and neglect, has revealed various functional difficulties beginning in childhood and persisting into adulthood (e.g., De Bellis, 2005; Gauthier, Stollak, Messé, & Aronoff, 1996; Glaser, 2000; Grassi-Oliveira & Stein, 2008; Kessler et al., 2010; Spertus, Yehuda, Wong, Halligan, & Seremetis, 2003; Sperry & Widom, 2013; Widom, 2000). These problems include cognitive impairments and lower intellectual functioning (De Bellis, Hooper, Spratt, & Woolley, 2009; Joseph, 1999; Strathearn, Gray, O'Callaghan, & Wood, 2001; Widom, 2000), psychopathology (Gauthier et al., 1996; Kessler et al., 2010; Powers, Ressler, & Bradley, 2009; Spertus et al., 2003; Widom, 2000), lower levels of interpersonal skills and support (Kim & Cicchetti, 2010; Sperry & Widom, 2013), impairments in emotion identification and regulation (De Bellis, 2005; Kim & Cicchetti, 2010; Pechtel & Pizzagalli, 2011), and physical health concerns (Moxley, Squires, & Lindstrom, 2012; Stirling & Amaya-Jackson, 2008; Walker et al., 1999), among others. Both direct and indirect pathways have been proposed to account for problems in adjustment in adulthood, which may stem from early childhood neglect. Most explanatory models consider not just the role of the abusive or neglectful acts themselves, but also take into account the influence of the family of origin (Gold, 2000; Widom, 2000), which may be due to the impact of the child's perception of parenting behaviors—or lack thereof.

Consequences of Neglect on Childhood and Adult Intellectual Functioning

As was discussed in Chap. 2, early childhood neglect has adverse implications for neurological development and functioning across several domains (e.g., social, emotional, cognitive). These neurological changes are evident in early childhood behavior, such that children from neglectful homes often present with lower intellectual functioning within the first 2 years of life (e.g., Strathearn et al., 2001). Impairments in cognitive development have been associated with differing subtypes of neglect, such as inadequate nutrition, lack of a stimulating environment (Moxley et al., 2012), and emotional neglect (Perry, 2002). As a result, neglected children often exhibit developmental delays and learning disabilities, especially when the absence of care occurs within the first 2 years of the child's life (Moxley et al., 2012). Moreover, in a prospective study comparing cases of substantiated childhood neglect in Black, White, and Hispanic individuals to matched controls, the authors found significant negative consequences for Black and White neglected children, with Hispanic children trending towards significance (Widom et al., 2012). These results suggest that childhood neglect may prove a risk factor for decreased intellectual capacities in individuals who experienced childhood neglect, regardless of race. However, when provided with early intervention and removed from the impoverished environment, neglected children have been found to recoup intellectual capacities (Perry, 2002).

In both children and adults, sustained cognitive impairments associated with neglect can contribute to lower intellectual functioning. For instance, in a prospective study examining risk factors and cognitive outcomes in low birth weight infants exposed to child maltreatment at age four, Strathearn et al. (2001) found that when considering physical abuse, emotional abuse, and neglect, neglect was the only maltreatment subtype that was independently associated with cognitive delays. Based on these results, it appears that, although overt subtypes of abuse have indisputably been associated with myriad problems in adulthood, with regard to cognitive functioning, neglect seems to have more detrimental effects than other kinds of "active" abuse or maltreatment. In addition, in a sample of adults with confirmed cases of childhood abuse and neglect, the majority of abused and neglected adults produced an intelligence quotient (IQ) below the average range, and significantly lower than the IQ of the comparison group (Widom, 2000). Additionally, the abuse and neglect survivors have been found to report fewer years of schooling (Walker et al., 1999; Widom, 2000) and lower-level employment when compared to individuals without histories of abuse or neglect (Widom, 2000). Considered jointly, impaired intellectual functioning associated with childhood neglect might reduce the likelihood of successfully completing high school and obtaining gainful employment. Other identified cognitive impairments include problems with attention and concentration (De Bellis, 2005; De Bellis et al., 2009) and impaired executive functioning (e.g., memory, decision making, emotion regulation) (De Bellis, 2005).

Neurological changes associated with childhood neglect also have implications for psychopathology. For example, construing neglect as a traumatic experience can manifest as anxiety and posttraumatic stress disorder (PTSD) in childhood, which may include difficulties concentrating and remembering (De Bellis et al., 2009). Additionally, emotional neglect has been associated with an increased risk for developing schizophrenia as related to decreased grey matter volume (Cancel et al., 2015).

Impact of Neglect on Adult Psychopathology

The World Health Organization found that, across several countries of varying income statuses, childhood adversity—that is, the presence of physical abuse, sexual abuse, neglect, interpersonal loss, parental maladjustment, economic adversity, and physical illness—predicted adult psychopathology (Kessler et al., 2010). More specifically, in adult survivors of childhood maltreatment and neglect, empirical studies have identified the presence of numerous mood, behavioral, and substance-related disorders (Gauthier et al., 1996; Kessler et al., 2010; Spertus et al., 2003; Widom, 2000).

It is well established that adults reporting a history of childhood abuse and neglect often experience depression and anxiety, a trend that has also been validated in adult survivors with a documented history of childhood abuse and/or neglect (e.g., Sperry & Widom, 2013; Widom et al., 2012), women in a community sample (Spertus et al., 2003), and college students (Gauthier et al., 1996). For instance, in comparing individuals of various races with a substantiated history of childhood neglect to matched control groups, White children showed the most pronounced negative mental health consequences when compared to Black and Hispanic children (Widom et al., 2012). Specifically, the authors found that White children were at an increased risk for mood disorders (i.e., dysthymia, major depressive disorder) and PTSD, as well as antisocial personality disorder and conduct disorder; Black children were at an increased risk for dysthymia and anxiety disorders (i.e., generalized anxiety disorder); and Hispanic children were at an increased risk for alcohol problems (Widom et al., 2012). Additionally, these results are further bolstered by a study examining a sample of adult women seeking services within a primary care setting (Spertus et al., 2003). Although some of the adult women reported co-occurring types of abuse, the outcomes of the study remained significant when controlling for the presence of physical and sexual abuse (Spertus et al., 2003). In fact, the literature suggests that neglect may be a stronger predictor of some psychological difficulties when compared to other types of maltreatment, such as physical abuse, an outcome that might be attributable to feelings of psychological abandonment associated with neglectful parenting (Gauthier et al., 1996). Lastly, when assessing adult psychological functioning in college students, neglect was independently associated with anxiety, depression, and somatization (Gauthier et al., 1996). This finding may prove especially significant, as there is a certain degree of resiliency inherent in having a history of childhood abuse or neglect and being successful in matriculating at the college level.

Regarding the adult risk for depression in a highly traumatized population, emotional abuse and neglect were stronger predictors than sexual or physical abuse (Powers et al., 2009). Additionally, the gender of the caregiver has also been identified as having a unique impact on the development of later psychopathology. For example, survivors of emotional neglect by a primary female caregiver in childhood experience greater psychological distress in adulthood when compared to survivors exposed to emotional neglect by a male caregiver or no neglect at all (Wark, Kruczek, & Boley, 2003). Considered jointly, these findings denote that the negative impact of neglect can produce mental health difficulties both in the absence of other forms of abuse and despite the covert nature of this maltreatment subtype.

Neglect has also been associated with eating pathology. According to a recent meta-analysis conducted by Pignatelli, Wampers, Loriedo, Biondi, and Vanderlinden (2016), the presence of childhood neglect (i.e., emotional and physical neglect) has been found in approximately 50% of individuals endorsing the presence of an eating disorder. Moreover, it is noted that the prevalence of neglect is greater in individuals with a history of eating disorders as compared to the general population (Pignatelli et al., 2016).

The relationship between neglect and substance use behaviors in adulthood is less consistently supported by the extant literature. For instance, research has shown that childhood adversity is associated with adult substance use behaviors (e.g., Felitti et al., 1998; Gerra et al., 2014; Kessler et al., 2010; Shin, Miller, & Teicher, 2013). Gerra et al. (2014) found that in a sample of male heroin users maintaining abstinence, perception of parental care and support in childhood was associated with substance abuse severity and the ability to cope with difficult emotional experiences in adulthood (Gerra et al., 2014). However, when examining childhood abuse and neglect in the absence of other adversities, it has been suggested that substance abuse problems appear more contingent on parental alcohol and drug abuse (Widom, 2000). Conversely, more recent studies have revealed a relationship between early life stress and substance dependence, such that men and women exposed to childhood maltreatment are at a greater risk for developing a substance use disorder (Enoch, 2011). Moreover, a longitudinal study found a greater increase of heavy episodic drinking beginning in adolescence, and continuing into young adulthood among individuals reporting a history of childhood neglect and physical abuse (Shin et al., 2013). This trend in drinking behavior was significant even after controlling for common substance abuse risk factors, such as parental and peer alcohol use, and depression (Shin et al., 2013). Consequently, given the undisputed role of parental substance abuse as an identified contextual risk factor for neglect (Barth, 2009; Copps Hartley, 2002; Evans, Garner, & Honig, 2014; Hobbs & Wynne, 2002; Moxley et al., 2012), as well as more current literature highlighting the relationship between childhood maltreatment and neglect, substance use behaviors in individuals with a history of perceived childhood neglect should be carefully assessed.

The development of posttraumatic stress disorder (PTSD) is often associated with the presence of childhood abuse, although not all survivors of trauma develop the disorder (Paris, 2013). The definition of childhood neglect does not strictly adhere to the *Diagnostic and Statistical Manual for Mental Disorders, Fifth Edition* (DSM-5; American Psychiatric Association, 2013) criteria for what constitutes a trauma exposure. However, several studies have provided evidence suggesting that survivors of a neglectful family of origin may present with PTSD and related functional impairments (Spertus et al., 2003). That is, although not an overt form of childhood maltreatment, children subjected to neglect and deprivation of care can perceive the experience as traumatic and may develop PTSD in the absence of a more clearly identified trauma (De Bellis et al., 2009). For instance, Grassi-Oliveira and Stein (2008) examined the relative impact of emotional and physical neglect as predictors of PTSD, over and above other forms of childhood maltreatment in a sample of low-income males and females in Brazil. Results demonstrated that neglect contributed to the later development of PTSD, specifically in adults who experienced neglect of emotional needs as compared to neglect of physical needs (Grassi-Oliveira & Stein, 2008). In the same vein, research controlling for the presence of physical and sexual abuse, as well as the number of total lifetime traumas, found that emotional abuse and neglect was significantly correlated with PTSD, among other psychiatric problems, in adult women presenting in a primary care setting (Spertus et al., 2003). In considering the aforementioned studies, it is evident that, despite non-adherence with the DSM-5 criteria outlining what constitutes a traumatic event, not having fundamental needs met in childhood is associated with trauma-related symptoms in adulthood. This is further evidenced by the presence of associated features of PTSD, such as interpersonal problems and impaired emotion regulation.

Similarly, neglect is associated with increased risk for personality disorders in adolescents and young adults (Johnson, Smailes, Cohen, Brown, & Bernstein, 2000). For instance, Johnson et al. (2000) conducted a community-based longitudinal study in which they interviewed 738 families (youths and their mothers) regarding their experiences with psychiatric symptomatology and experiences of cognitive, emotional, physical and supervision neglect. Their findings suggest that cognitive neglect was not associated with increased risk for personality disorders; however, emotional neglect increased youths' risk for paranoid and avoidant personality disorders, physical neglect was associated with narcissistic and schizotypal personality disorders, and supervision neglect was associated with borderline, paranoid, and passive aggressive personality disorder symptoms (Johnson et al., 2000). While child neglect can negatively affect personality development, it is important to note that not all neglected children exhibit symptoms of personality disorders, suggesting that protective factors and resiliency moderate the impact of neglect on personality development.

Interpersonal Problems and Impaired Emotion Regulation

Insufficient parenting and modeling of ineffective parental behaviors can contribute to maladaptive or developmentally inappropriate ways of coping (e.g., impulsive behavior; Widom, 2000) and ineffective interpersonal styles of relating to and communicating with others (Joseph, 1999; Kim & Cicchetti, 2010; Maheu et al., 2010). As outlined in Chap. 3, neglect has adverse consequences on attachment formation and has been associated with interpersonal difficulties in both childhood (e.g., Kim & Cicchetti, 2010) and adulthood (e.g., Gauthier et al., 1996). The presence of internalizing and externalizing behaviors has been noted, as well as problems with emotion regulation and negative peer relationships in neglected children ages 6–12 (Kim & Cicchetti, 2010). For example, the authors proposed that negative social relationships might be associated with ineffective parental modeling of perspective-taking skills aimed at fostering appropriate empathy and emotional awareness. The inadequate transmission of these skills may contribute to the development of aggressive behaviors in maltreated children (Kim & Cicchetti, 2010). Physically neglected children are more likely to be rejected by their peers, and peer rejection has been found to mediate the relationship between physical neglect and violent behaviors in adolescence (Chapple, Tyler, & Bersani, 2005).

Childhood neglect (i.e., physical and emotional neglect) has been found to be negatively correlated with perceived family support and perceived friend support on retrospective report (Powers et al., 2009). Moreover, low levels of perceived support in adulthood may be associated with deficient interpersonal skills in people who experienced childhood neglect when compared to non-maltreated controls (Sperry & Widom, 2013). Consequently, neglected children and adults may experience lower levels of support, thereby reinforcing attachment insecurity and reducing the likelihood for corrective social interactions. However, perceived friend support appears to be associated with lower levels of depression when accounting for child abuse and neglect, suggesting that the perception of support may mitigate the development of later psychopathology in this population. It was notable, however, that tests of gender differences revealed that support may only buffer against the development of depression in females (Powers et al., 2009).

Difficulties maintaining support in childhood may also be related to stress accompanied by the abuse, which can erode relationships over time (Sperry & Widom, 2013). Ineffective family environments are often characterized by low levels of cohesion, independence, and expressiveness, and high levels of conflict and control (Gold, 2000; Gold, Hyman, & Andres-Hyman, 2004). Therefore, children of abuse and neglect may feel unable to disclose their at-home interactions with others, contributing to withdrawal and avoidance of other experiences. This may be further compounded due to the child's perception of family support, given the likelihood that the maltreatment occurred within the home (Powers et al., 2009). Additionally, in adulthood, individuals with a history of child maltreatment and neglect have been found to have higher rates of divorce (Widom, 2000) and lower rates of marriage (Walker et al., 1999) when compared to non-maltreated counterparts. Higher rates of marital discord may lend credence to interpersonal difficulties and attachment insecurity. Nevertheless, due to difficulties maintaining support, the presence of social support in adult survivors of childhood maltreatment has been identified as a protective factor to adult anxiety and depression (Sperry & Widom, 2013). Specifically, the authors postulate that the development of one healthy relationship may buffer the effects of ineffective parenting (Sperry & Widom, 2013).

Chronic abuse and neglect are likely to have a pervasive impact on a child's regulatory processes, such as emotion regulation (Glaser, 2000; Pechtel & Pizzagalli, 2011) and emotion identification (Young & Widom, 2014). Although the onset of emotion dysregulation may be in response to childhood stressors and adversities, affective impairments may persist into adulthood and contribute to the development of psychopathology (Pechtel & Pizzagalli, 2011). For example, relative to comparison youths, those with a history of caregiver deprivation and emotional neglect exhibited difficulties in identifying emotional expressions (Maheu et al., 2010) and distinguishing between emotional expressions (Kim & Cicchetti, 2010). These impairments are attributed in part to adverse neurological development associated with neglect (Joseph, 1999; Tanner & Turney, 2003), specifically in the amygdala (Bogdan, Williamson, & Hariri, 2012; Pechtel & Pizzagalli, 2011). These results were further supported by a prospective study of emotion processing in individuals with a documented history of childhood maltreatment (Young & Widom, 2014).

Findings suggest that individuals with a history of childhood abuse and/or neglect exhibit deficits in processing positive emotions, possibly due to a negative worldview developed from chronic childhood adversity or having experienced less positive emotions growing up (Young & Widom, 2014). Lastly, impaired emotion regulation associated with deficient parenting behaviors in childhood may also be related to the higher rate of eating disorders in adulthood. That is, restrictive or purging behaviors may have been adopted as a means to modulate emotional responses to obtain a sense of external control (Pignatelli et al., 2016).

Outcomes on Physical Health

A childhood history characterized by emotional abuse and neglect may also have implications for health care utilization (e.g., Spertus et al., 2003; Stirling & Amaya-Jackson, 2008) and physical health in adulthood (Nikulina & Widom, 2014). This may be particularly relevant due to the presence of somatic complains and poor self-care (Spertus et al., 2003). For instance, women with a history of child abuse and maltreatment were more likely to identify their health as fair or poor when compared to those without an abuse history (Walker et al., 1999). These women were also more likely to engage in health risk behaviors (e.g., driving while under the influence) and suffer from obesity (Walker et al., 1999). Compared with women who did not have a history of childhood abuse or neglect, those who did had significantly greater levels of functional disability, and more physical symptoms and diagnoses (Walker et al., 1999). Additional support for an association between childhood neglect and adult physical health comes from a prospective cohort design study, utilizing data examining race, childhood neglect, and childhood family and neighborhood poverty (Nikulina & Widom, 2014). Results revealed that childhood neglect in combination with race and poverty factors predicted poorer pulmonary functioning in adulthood (Nikulina & Widom, 2014). The authors posit that the interaction effect of the examined variables may speak to children's resilience when faced with childhood neglect, and emphasize the importance of protective factors (Nikulina & Widom, 2014). In summary, child abuse, neglect, and other adversities have been linked to serious health consequences, including stroke, cancer, heart disease (Stirling & Amaya-Jackson, 2008), and poorer lung functioning (Nikulina & Widom, 2014).

The Impact of Neglect on Occupational Functioning and Offending

As has been outlined above, childhood maltreatment has been associated with problems in cognitive functioning (Strathearn et al., 2001; Walker et al., 1999; Widom, 2000), fewer years of schooling (Walker et al., 1999; Widom, 2000), impaired emotion regulation (Glaser, 2000; Pechtel & Pizzagalli, 2011; Young & Widom, 2014) and interpersonal functioning (Joseph, 1999; Kim & Cicchetti, 2010; Maheu et al., 2010), and psychopathology (Gauthier et al., 1996; Kessler et al., 2010; Spertus et al., 2003; Widom, 2000), any of which, alone, may have implications for occupational functioning in adulthood. However, efforts to assess the impact of adverse childhood experiences on ability to sustain employment in adulthood have recently been independently evaluated (Fahy et al., 2017). Researchers in the United Kingdom found that, in a longitudinal study of adults who reported having been abused or neglected during childhood, there was a greater likelihood that they reported permanent sickness or disability at age 55, resulting in reduced labor force participation (Fahy et al., 2017). These findings suggest that the presence of childhood maltreatment can affect an individual's ability to sustain employment in adulthood independent of other types of impairment.

Childhood neglect has also been implicated in arrests for juvenile offenses and violent behaviors, in adults of differing ethnic groups (i.e., Whites, Blacks, and Hispanics) when comparing individuals with a documented history of childhood neglect to matched controls; effects that were especially in Blacks (Widom et al., 2012). Widom et al. (2012) found that neglected Black children were more than twice as likely to be arrested for violence when compared to matched controls, a trend that was not found in Whites, although neglected White children reported engaging in more violence than Black children (and White controls). In contrast, Hispanic individuals with a documented history of neglect were at a reduced risk for having been arrested for a violent crime as a juvenile or adult when compared to Hispanic controls (Widom et al., 2012).

Summary

The extant literature has consistently revealed the negative effects of childhood neglect across several domains, including social, occupational, and functional impairment. As a result, it is evident that childhood neglect of varying subtypes is related to impaired emotion processing (Young & Widom, 2014) and regulation (Maheu et al., 2010). Additionally, deficits in functioning associated with neglect have also been attributed to psychopathology including PTSD (De Bellis et al., 2009; Grassi-Oliveira & Stein, 2008; Spertus et al., 2003), somatic symptoms (Gauthier et al., 1996; Spertus et al., 2003), depression (Gauthier et al., 1996; Sperry & Widom, 2013; Spertus et al., 2003), anxiety (Gauthier et al., 1996; Sperry & Widom, 2013; Spertus et al., 2003), eating disorders (Pignatelli et al., 2016), and substance abuse disorders (Enoch, 2011; Gerra et al., 2014; Shin et al., 2013).

Chapter 5
Assessment, Prevention, and Treatment

As previously established, childhood neglect often co-occurs with other child maltreatment, thus making it difficult to identify or assess. Moreover, the lack of agreement about what constitutes minimally acceptable standards of childcare, coupled with uncertainty as to the point at which subpar parenting has adverse consequences to child development, contributes to difficulty in assessing for neglectful parenting behavior (Howard & Brooks-Gunn, 2009; McDaniel & Dillenburger, 2007). That is, certain parenting behaviors may not legally be defined as neglect (e.g., leaving a child of a certain age at home without supervision), yet can have damaging effects on the child. Perhaps due, in part, to difficulties in the recognition of childhood neglect, efforts to improve surveillance of subthreshold parenting have been most frequently discussed in the literature by way of primary prevention (e.g., Evans, Garner, & Honig, 2014), such that established programs (e.g., home-visiting programs) aim to provide support to at-risk families prior to any indication of neglect or abuse to the child. It is also important to consider that different subtypes of neglect may require different types of prevention and treatment efforts (Straus & Kantor, 2005).

Assessment

Increasing early detection of childhood neglect and abuse requires three aspects of assessment (Caldwell, Bogat, & Davidson, 1988). The first step involves identifying potential perpetrators and victims through careful consideration of individual and contextual risk factors, as well as theoretical underpinnings of child maltreatment. Commonly observed risk factors include poverty (Caldwell et al., 1988; Evans et al., 2014; Moxley, Squires, & Lindstrom, 2012); parental substance abuse (Copps Hartley, 2002; Hobbs & Wynne, 2002; Moxley et al., 2012), young maternal age, unwanted pregnancy, lack of prenatal care (Evans et al., 2014), single parent households (Evans et al., 2014; Moxley et al., 2012), and parental mental illness

(Hobbs & Wynne, 2002; Moxley et al., 2012). The severity of risk factors might be considered simultaneously with the presence of protective factors (e.g., motivation to change, level of available support). Next, those individuals who have been identified as being at risk as perpetrators or victims are compared to those believed to be less at risk. Although previous attempts have been made to identify characteristics of potential perpetrators through the use of the Minnesota Multiphasic Personality Inventory (MMPI), those efforts have been unsuccessful (Caldwell et al., 1988). Additionally, in a study examining videotaped recordings of caregiver-child interactions, the length of time of positive interactions between the caregiver and child has been found to predict neglect, in that shorter-duration positive engagements at age three were associated with increased risk for neglect at age four (Dishion et al., 2015).

Third, when assessing for child maltreatment and neglect through the use of specific assessment measures, the predictive validity of the measures being implemented must be carefully evaluated (Caldwell et al., 1988). That is, when assessing for risk of neglect, self-report inventories, behavior rating scales, and observational instruments may provide valuable information about parenting attitudes and parent-child interactions and relational patterns. However, how these measures predict neglect or maltreatment must also be evaluated. For example, the Child Abuse Potential Inventory is one of the most commonly utilized assessments (CAPI; Milner, 1994); however, this measure estimates the potential for abuse rather than incidence rate (Evans et al., 2014). This suggests that, although the CAPI can provide information regarding the likelihood of whether or not a parent may perpetrate child maltreatment, it does not produce an indication as to whether or not abuse or neglect has already occurred.

In addition to administering various measures, a structured interview should be conducted when neglect is suspected. If the interview indeed reveals the presence of neglect, investigators should consider why the parents are failing (e.g., lack of understanding of positive parenting or child development), whether or not they are motivated to change, and how they can be better supported (e.g., peers, extended family; Hobbs & Wynne, 2002). Moreover, investigators should directly inquire as to parents' behaviors towards their children (Howard & Brooks-Gunn, 2009). Depending upon the risk factors present within each family system, parents may be unaware of how certain behaviors may have adverse effects on their child's development due to limited resources and knowledge of the developmental process. For example, parents may be unable to afford early educational opportunities and may themselves exhibit a diminished capacity for reading. This combination of an impoverished environment and reduced cognitive capacities in parents may contribute to future cognitive difficulties in the child.

Considering the utility of these steps in uncovering childhood neglect, ensuing intervention strategies should be geared towards educating community members—or at a minimum mandated reporters (e.g., psychologists, school psychologists, teachers)—of contextual risk factors and the importance of observed changes in child behaviors and other evaluative measures to improve the assessment of child neglect. For instance, primary health care providers may play an integral role in identifying children being reared in an impoverished environment. This may be noted through a failure to thrive, or the development of maladaptive patterns of behaviors associated with neglect or maltreatment. As a result, physicians may be successful in educating parents on strategies aimed at stress reduction within their children (Stirling & Amaya-Jackson, 2008). Consequently, various prevention and intervention programs may be implemented to target specific individual difficulties within at-risk families to mitigate the vulnerability of the family system to neglect.

Primary and Secondary Prevention

For prevention efforts to be successful, children and families most at risk for child maltreatment must be identified early (Evans et al., 2014; Guterman, 1997; Howard & Brooks-Gunn, 2009; McDaniel & Dillenburger, 2007). To better support these efforts, the Child Abuse Prevention and Treatment Act (CAPTA) was established in 1974 and has undergone several revisions (i.e., 2003, 2010) to provide funding for prevention and treatment services for children at risk for child abuse and neglect (Moxley et al., 2012).

Primary prevention programs aim to prevent new cases of child maltreatment from occurring by identifying maladaptive ecological systems and parent-child interactions (Guterman, 1997). Through identifying these risk factors, parents are able to learn about effective parenting behaviors and means of coping with normal developmental and problem child behaviors. In a review of the literature, Guterman (1997) identified several commonalities among prevention programs, which included early identification and screening of at-risk families (e.g., young mothers) and initiation of services in the perinatal period or shortly after birth. In addition, programs that promote health are examples of primary prevention programs (Wekerle & Wolfe, 1993). By identifying families through focusing on health and wellness, the stigma associated with assessment of abuse and neglect potential is diminished, thereby resulting in families being more amenable to actively seeking and receiving services. Further, in directing prevention efforts at families free from abuse and neglect, the implementation of such programs should demonstrate a reduction in the incidence rate of child maltreatment when compared to families without such programs (Caldwell et al., 1988).

Primary prevention programs can encompass a variety of strategies to bolster protective factors among at-risk parents and children (Wekerle & Wolfe, 1993). For instance, success has been found in implementing parenting skills programs where parents learn strategies for feeding and bathing their children (McDaniel & Dillenburger, 2007), as well as psychoeducation on child development and behavioral techniques for problem behaviors (Evans et al., 2014; Mikton & Butchart, 2009). In addition, there has been support for home-visiting programs across multiple studies (e.g., Evans et al., 2014; MacMillon et al., 2005, Mikton & Butchart, 2009) especially among first-time mothers, thereby providing the most valid indication of successful primary prevention programs (Howard & Brooks-Gunn, 2009).

Table 5.1 Overview of child maltreatment prevention programs and interventions (Mikton & Butchart, 2009)

Intervention/ Program	Goal	Results
Parent education programs (group format)	Improve child-rearing skills and knowledge of child development	Mixed reviews: two meta-analyses reported small-medium effect; one meta-analysis reported a lack of support for effectiveness.
Multi-component interventions	Provide family support, child care and early childhood education, and parenting skills	Mixed reviews: one meta-analysis reported a medium-large effect size in support of the intervention; two meta-analyses reported mixed or insufficient support for the intervention.
Media-based interventions	Increase public awareness of child maltreatment risk factors	Mixed reviews: one meta-analysis reported a large effect size in support of the intervention; two meta-analyses revealed mixed or insufficient support for the intervention.
Support/mutual aid (group format)	Increase parents' social support systems	Mixed reviews: one review found a small-medium effect; one review deemed the intervention ineffective.
Abusive head trauma prevention	Aim to reduce shaken baby/infant syndrome and reduce the incidence of traumatic brain injury	Mixed reviews: one meta-analysis reported a reduction in abusive head trauma; one meta-analysis deemed the program ineffective.
Home visitation programs	Provide family support, improve knowledge of child development, connect family members to additional services, as needed	Mixed reviews; however, surveillance bias and methodological problems may contribute to an increase in reports to child protective services agencies, thereby reducing the effectiveness of the program

Several reviews have been conducted identifying commonly employed prevention programs, goals, and outcomes. See Table 5.1 for a summary of a review conducted by Mikton and Butchart (2009) outlining several early interventions aimed to prevent child maltreatment.

Home-visitation programs appear to be among the most frequently researched prevention programs. Many of these programs aim to initiate services during pregnancy. For instance, Olds et al. (1997) examined the long-term effects of a home-visitation program when services were rendered during the prenatal and early childhood period to first time mothers presenting with various risk factors (e.g., low SES, young age) and no history of child abuse or neglect. Additional programs have been developed to prevent subsequent incidences of abuse in families already involved with child protective services while still maintaining custody of their children (MacMillon et al., 2005). A review of the literature on home-visiting programs revealed that, although the degree of training of nurses or paraprofessionals and intensity of the home-visits varies across studies (Howard & Brooks-Gunn, 2009), those services provided within the context of the family's home typically result in positive outcomes, such as improved parenting behaviors and child well-being (Howard & Brooks-Gunn, 2009). As outlined in Table 5.1, home-visiting programs have several functions, including modifying parenting behaviors and providing support and psychoeducation (Howard & Brooks-Gunn, 2009; Mikton & Butchart, 2009). Moreover, given that infants are at the greatest risk for abuse and neglect, perinatal intervention is ideal (Howard & Brooks-Gunn, 2009).

Regarding secondary prevention programs, services are targeted to at-risk populations (Guterman, 1997), including families where societal factors that foster abusive behavior are evident (Wekerle & Wolfe, 1993), such as negative parenting attitudes. Although both primary and secondary prevention programs aim to reduce or prevent the likelihood of abusive or neglectful parenting, secondary prevention programs may contribute to a refinement of identification and assessment of childhood maltreatment due to targeting families in which such parenting behaviors have been previously noted (Guterman, 1997).

Assessing the Effectiveness of Prevention Programs

As outlined briefly in Table 5.1, many of the reviews examining the effectiveness of the various prevention efforts have yielded mixed results, making it difficult to draw definitive conclusions regarding the impact of the aforementioned preventive programs. Assessing for the effectiveness of preventive programs is complicated by several methodological issues, including identifying the target populations to be serviced, determining the types of interventions that should be implemented, and appropriately allocating funding within these programs (Wekerle & Wolfe, 1993). It is probable that these issues are related, such that a more definitive identification of potential perpetrators and victims can facilitate narrowing efficacious interventions and reducing costs. Additionally, research examining prevention efforts is mixed, but these efforts yield improvements in family functioning that range from minor to significant (Howard & Brooks-Gunn, 2009; Mikton & Butchart, 2009). Future research should aim to more rigorously assess the effectiveness of preventive programs by delivering such services to the general population (Caldwell et al., 1988).

Home-visiting programs have been found to increase the duration of positive interactions within the caregiver-child dyad, thereby reducing parental neglect (Dishion et al., 2015). Although meta-analyses of home-visiting programs reveal modest effects, the heterogeneity across studies suggests that definitive conclusions should be made with caution. The variability across studies includes the degree of training among those delivering the intervention (e.g., nurse, paraprofessional), the clarity of curriculum and amount of structure being implemented within the family, and outcomes being evaluated (Howard & Brooks-Gunn, 2009). To make future studies more methodologically sound, credentials of those entering the home and delivering services should be consistent and a curriculum with a high degree of fidelity should be established (Howard & Brooks-Gunn, 2009). Furthermore, modest effects of home-visitation programs might be due to surveillance bias among families receiving home-visiting services as compared to families receiving no intervention. That is, nurses and paraprofessionals in the home of suspected

Table 5.2 Overview of parent training and education programs (Barth, 2009)

Program	Targeted risk factor	Goal
Focus on Families (FOF)	Substance use	Emphasizes relapse prevention for mothers on methadone maintenance; provides parenting skills education and case management
Arkansas Center for Addiction Research, Education, and Services (CARES)	Substance use	Provides residential prevention and treatment to pregnant women, mothers, and children; provides parenting classes which emphasize appropriate parental roles and positive discipline
Coalition on Addiction, Pregnancy, and Parenting (CAPP)	Substance use	Provides residential treatment and parenting skills groups, which also includes psychoeducation on child development and a mothers' support group
Thresholds Mothers' Project (TMP)	Mental illness	Provides services to mothers and children; facilitates gaining supportive and independent housing and enrolling children in educational programs
Child-parent psychotherapy	Domestic violence	Focuses on strengthening the relationship and communication and reducing child behavioral problems
Incredible Years (IY)	Child conduct problems	Provides services to both children and parents; teaches effective parenting techniques
Parent-Child Interaction Therapy (PCIT)	Child conduct problems	Provides feedback to the parent through observation of parent-child interactions; teaches proper attending techniques to child's behaviors and other skills
Triple P- Positive Parenting Program	Multifaceted	Includes five levels of intervention based on social learning theory, including different methods of rendering services; utilizes home visits to ensure implementation of skills

perpetrators or at-risk parents have more observational opportunities for parent-child interactions, thereby increasing the likelihood that an appropriate report would be made to a child protection agency if questionable behaviors are noted (Howard & Brooks-Gunn, 2009; Mikton & Butchart, 2009).

Parent education programs have also gained traction in prevention efforts (see Table 5.2 for overview). These programs have been directed at shaping realistic expectations for child behaviors and appropriate ways of responding to those behaviors (Barth, 2009). Due to the impact of parental substance use on child neglect, several programs have been developed specifically to support parents with these difficulties (Barth, 2009). For instance, Focus on Families (FOF) and the Arkansas Center for Addiction Research, Education, and Services (CARES) both provide services to substance-using mothers. Women who seek such services during the perinatal period of their pregnancy may reduce the likelihood that their children are born addicted to substances, which is often associated with cognitive deficits and more problem child behaviors (Barth, 2009). As a result, targeting maternal substance use while simultaneously teaching appropriate parenting skills can ultimately reduce the burden of stress on these mothers, thus attenuating the risk of child maltreatment and neglect (Barth, 2009). More generally, parenting training programs are often most effective when a variety of services are delivered that are specifically targeted to the parents' needs, typically including a home-visitation component (Barth, 2009). For example, a first-time mother may benefit from more general parent training including feeding, bathing, and child development, whereas a mother with a child presenting with behavioral problems may benefit from parent training regarding ways of establishing consistency within the home and effective forms of discipline (e.g., token economy system).

Reporting Neglect

Reporting laws for child abuse and neglect exist in all 50 states and the U.S. territories, although what is characterized as abuse or neglect may differ from state to state (US Department of Health and Human Services, 2013). Similarly, who is deemed a mandated reporter may change across states. Typically, mandated reporters include medical professionals, law enforcement officers, mental health practitioners, and teachers (US Department of Health and Human Services, 2013); however, in some states, such as Florida, any person who knows or has reasonable cause to suspect abuse or neglect is considered a mandated reporter (Florida Abuse Hotline, 2013). Reports of abuse can be made anonymously, except when the report is made by a mandated reporter, at which point the reporter's name is documented (Florida Abuse Hotline, 2013). Suspected or known incidents of neglect can be made by contacting local Child Protective Services agencies and knowledge of the suspected victim's whereabouts is imperative for effectively filing a report.

Treatment Interventions for Families Characterized by Neglect

Obtaining therapeutic intervention for child survivors of abuse and neglect is an important step to mitigating the effects of long-term sequelae. Due to the pervasiveness of poor family functioning in homes where neglect is present, treatment tends to be targeted to both children and their families (Allin, Wathen, & MacMillan, 2005). A review of the literature on treatment approaches for childhood neglect indicated the potential benefits of group play therapy and imaginative play training for children exposed to neglect in an effort to increase interactions with peers (Allin et al., 2005). Other programs offered to child survivors include therapeutic day treatment programs to facilitate cooperation with peers. Such programs have yielded improvements in social behavior, cognitive development, and self-concept when compared to children with a history of abuse and neglect receiving no intervention

(Wolfe & Wekerle, 1993). Additionally, trauma-related responses in neglected or maltreated children, such as hypervigilance, are often reinforced in early environments characterized by dysfunction. As a result, therapy for the abused or neglected child should attempt to restructure the child's pattern of thinking and emotional responding, while simultaneously providing parent training (Stirling & Amaya-Jackson, 2008).

Parent-focused behavioral interventions, as discussed above, tend to incorporate parent training, which often provide psychoeducation on managing problem child behavior as well as improving the parents' ability to cope with their own stressors (Wolfe & Wekerle, 1993). Taken together with cognitive-behavioral interventions, instilling a positive parenting attitude and effective coping and child rearing skills appear to be the most effective approaches for remediating the effects of neglect and abuse (Wolfe & Wekerle, 1993). Lastly, due to the impact of neglect on a child's cognitive capacities, identified children should be referred for neuropsychological assessments to determine whether or not any deficits exist (Watts-English, Fortson, Gibler, Hooper, & De Bellis, 2006). This will facilitate the identification of children already experiencing impairments in learning and provide them with appropriate support aimed at remediating such deficits.

Treatment for Adult Survivors of Neglect

Guidelines for the treatment of individuals who have experienced prolonged trauma specify a three-phased approach for ameliorating PTSD and trauma-related symptoms. Phase One requires that the client establish and maintain feelings of safety, and is often the longest phase of the process (Herman, 1997). Phase Two involves recalling traumatic experiences, a goal of which is twofold: (1) to empower the client and (2) to perceive and understand the trauma differently (Herman, 1997). In doing so, the client no longer identifies with the trauma in a self-loathing way and is able to construct a new interpretation of the event. This affords the opportunity for the client to successfully restructure negative cognitions, which may involve the way in which the client perceives and interacts with the world. Although processing of traumatic memories may prove beneficial for many clients, delving into traumatic memories may temporarily diminish the client's level of functioning; therefore, if recalling traumatic events, the client must be prepared to experience and effectively manage distress (Gold, 2000; Herman, 1997). When traumatic experiences are addressed prematurely and without safety being established, the client may feel revictimized through reinforcement of distorted beliefs about themselves (Gold, 2000; Herman, 1997). This impulsive remembrance of traumatic events may emerge due to the client's willingness to please others (i.e., the clinician) despite their not feeling comfortable disclosing their trauma. Although both authors agree that recalling these memories can be distressing and impairing, once the traumatic memories are no longer so intensely feared, they may no longer seem an integral part of the survivor's life or narrative. The third, and final, phase involves reintegration and is characterized by assimilating new interpretations of the trauma into daily interactions (Herman, 1997). Although Herman's three-phase model for trauma treatment is not directed specifically for individuals with a history of childhood neglect, this framework has been applied to subsequent treatments applied to those with prolonged childhood abuse and neglect.

In our search of the extant literature, we have found little, if any emphasis specifically on the treatment of childhood neglect. In fact, our search yielded one recent article stating, "no treatment model has been specifically designed to target the effects of childhood emotional abuse and neglect (Grossman, Spinazzola, Zucker, & Hopper, 2017, p. 87)." However, adult survivors of neglect may present with similar difficulties to those of prolonged childhood abuse, and as a result, may benefit from being provided with appropriate daily living skills to remediate any gaps in development that resulted from the ineffective family environment that contributed to subsequent difficulties (Gold, 2000). Contextual Trauma Therapy (CTT) (Gold, 2000) was initially developed for survivors of prolonged childhood abuse to accommodate deficits in adaptive coping skills and to provide an alternative to exclusively trauma-focused treatments. This model of treatment encompasses the three-phase model for trauma treatment, though deviates in that CTT acknowledges that processing of traumatic memories may not be necessary for resolving trauma-related symptoms in all clients. Instead, it suggests a more client-directed approach, where the client defines the issues that should be of focus of treatment. Further, CTT outlines that, as the symptoms that the client hopes to improve are diminished, the desire to address the trauma becomes less commanding. In this way, negative cognitions that exist within the client, which possibly emerged as a consequence of the trauma, are addressed without explicitly describing the traumatic experiences (Gold, 2000). When focusing less on the abuse, the client no longer feels the need to identify himself or herself as an abuse survivor, though this is not to say that exposure to traumatic memories is always unwarranted. Consequently, the model maintains that the majority of the therapy will be in the safety and stabilization phase (i.e., Phase One) in order to provide opportunities for a client-guided conceptualization, establish and maintain a strong, collaborative therapeutic relationship, and to facilitate therapist guided skills transmission.

The client-guided conceptualization serves to remind the client that he is the expert of his experiences and provides an opportunity for the client to enhance his understanding into the etiology and maintenance of problems in adjustment in adulthood. In this way, the therapist is following the client's lead, thereby providing opportunities for the client to reclaim her voice regarding her treatment and the trajectory of her life. The collaborative relationship serves to model a healthy and reciprocal relationship, which for many survivors of childhood abuse and neglect is a novel experience, occurring for the first time within the therapeutic context. Moreover, the collaborative relationship serves as a model for future relationships as it is characterized by earned trust, cooperation, collaboration, authenticity, and appropriate emotional reciprocity. Lastly, the therapist-guided skills transmission (e.g., pleasant activity scheduling, assertiveness training, grounding techniques) serves to teach evidence-based interventions aimed at remediating deficits in adult functioning. These three interrelated components are key to successful outcomes in survivors of prolonged childhood abuse and neglect and are implemented in an integrative, individualized treatment plan tailored to the survivor's needs at the current time.

To address the gap in the literature regarding treatment of childhood neglect and emotional abuse, Grossman et al. (2017) have proposed an evidence-informed model of treatment incorporating a phase-based approach and empirically supported interventions for trauma processing, a strong therapeutic alliance, and treatment of dissociation, referred to as component-based psychotherapy (CBP). Similar to CTT, CBP emphasizes and integrates the relational context between the client and therapist and establishment of regulatory skills (e.g., skill building techniques, grounding and relaxation techniques) (Gold, 2000; Grossman et al., 2017). Additionally, although discussed and relevant in CTT, CBP identifies a dissociative parts component processing of a trauma narrative as primary in the therapy (Grossman et al., 2017).

As is evident in the overlap between these two therapies, providing treatment for individuals of prolonged childhood abuse and neglect is multifaceted and requires consideration of various components in remedying difficulties stemming from childhood. Moreover, both CTT and CBP speak to the necessity of a genuine and empathic therapist to provide a corrective relational experience, facilitating healthy attachment formation, as well as providing skills of daily living to enhance regulatory processes and remediate childhood deficits impeding adulthood functioning.

Conclusions

Enhancing parenting skills and providing psychoeducation on childhood development, managing problem child behaviors, and forming effective parent-child relationships, can support at-risk parents in modifying their parenting behaviors and attitudes, thus reducing their risk for abusing and/or neglecting their children. As stated previously, a deeper understanding of child development can improve parent-child interactions and facilitate more appropriate responding to problem child behavior (Barth, 2009; Mikton & Butchart, 2009). Similarly, parenting psychoeducation programs and at-home visitation interventions may serve to revise parenting attitudes contributing to more positive behaviors directed towards their children. This is bolstered by the trend of treatment strategies focusing on promoting parental abilities (Wolfe & Wekerle, 1993). Perhaps the factor that best predicts success in preventive programs is the motivation of parents to stay involved and implement learned skills (Barth, 2009). This may suggest that techniques geared at increasing parents' motivation for change can improve parenting behavior and reduce the likelihood of abusive or neglectful behavior.

Chapter 6
Clinical Case Examples

As is evident from the previous chapters, childhood neglect is an insidious form of childhood maltreatment that can go undetected by both the untrained and trained eye, and can have negative implications across cognitive, emotional, interpersonal, and occupational domains. As a result, this chapter serves to illustrate the conceptualization and approach to treatment of several adult survivors of childhood neglect and co-occurring abuse.

Undetected Childhood Neglect

A 49-year-old Caucasian man, "David," was reared in a single-parent household. He was presenting for therapy for the treatment of persistent depressive disorder, generalized anxiety disorder and interpersonal difficulties. He expressed that he had been receiving disability for his mental health diagnoses for the last decade and had an interest in returning to work, although was concerned due to his limited education and difficulties maintaining consistent behaviors related to his chronic depression. David reported that his mother had a history of depression, suicide attempts, and alcohol abuse, and he described her as unaffectionate. David reported not having had a relationship with his father, indicating that his father died while David was in elementary school. He characterized his childhood environment as often being devoid of food and unsafe (e.g., mother left the stove on when intoxicated). He also disclosed academic difficulties, having few friends, and being bullied at school. David stated that, due to continued academic difficulties and a lack of parental supervision, he became truant and eventually dropped out of high school. However, despite his academic problems and frequent truancy, the school failed to inquire as to the status of David's home environment or intervene.

As is evident in the above case example, David experienced childhood emotional, physical, and supervision neglect. In conceptualizing this case utilizing

© The Author(s) 2018
N. A. Sciarrino et al., *Understanding Child Neglect*, SpringerBriefs in Psychology, https://doi.org/10.1007/978-3-319-74811-5_6

45

contextual trauma therapy (CTT) (Gold, 2000), early childhood neglect coupled with a deficient family of origin contributed to limited effective coping strategies, and subsequent mental health and interpersonal stressors in adulthood. Consequently, therapy utilizing CTT (Gold, 2000) sought to remediate deficits in skills of daily living through a combination of: (1) a client-guided exploration of the etiology and maintenance of difficulties in adulthood, (2) therapist-guided skills transmission (e.g., behavioral activation, mindfulness skills), and (3) the establishment of a strong, collaborative relationship.

Through the client-guided conceptualization, it was discovered that David's interpersonal difficulties were specific to his style of communicating with women, which he attributed to his mother's "cold" and "distant" demeanor growing up. Additionally, he expressed poor eating habits and limited self-care, and an inability to cope with daily stressors, associated with only having had access to unhealthy food options in his childhood home, and inappropriate modeling of coping, respectively. In considering the role of these subtypes of neglect and previous research examining the psychological and occupational sequelae associated with childhood neglect, it is unsurprising that David presented with chronic depressed mood (Widom et al., 2012) and other psychopathology, as well as limited formal education (Walker et al., 1999; Widom, 2000) and premature termination of employment associated with disability (Fahy et al., 2017). Skills emphasized with David in therapy included pleasant activity scheduling to increase behavioral activation and reduce depressive symptoms, as well as psychoeducation into cognitive distortions and cognitive restructuring to target anxiety. Dialectical Behavioral Therapy (DBT) skills (Linehan, 2015) were also employed to facilitate mindfulness and reduce ruminative patterns of thinking, distress tolerance to increase acceptance when experiencing discomfort, and interpersonal effectiveness skills to enhance an effective communication style. Lastly, the therapeutic alliance served to model a secure attachment, such that the therapist provided a consistent and safe environment, where David was able to establish and maintain clear expectations for the therapist's behaviors. Additionally, working with a female therapist allowed David to explore inappropriate relational patterns with women, while providing a corrective and supportive experience interacting with a woman.

Childhood Neglect as a Precursor to Subsequent Abuse

A 54-year-old Caucasian woman, "Sally," was reared in a single family house and was the youngest of four siblings, all of whom were at least 8 years older than she. She presented for treatment with symptoms of PTSD and depression stemming from childhood sexual abuse and neglect. Sally expressed that her life difficulties revolved around her feeling as though her mother "never loved [her]" and that she was "never good enough for anyone." Sally expressed that her mother was depressed and often left Sally on her own. As a toddler, Sally's mother allowed her to go live with a neighbor, as she "could not handle being a mother." When Sally returned home, her mother was distant, detached and was not affectionate with her. Sally also reported that her mother did not provide adequate supervision and she was often left to come and go as she pleased. She began babysitting for a family at age 11, where she was responsible for four young children. Sally explained that the father of that family began to sexually abuse her, and the abuse continued for approximately 4 years. To cope with her depression and shame, she began to abuse alcohol at age 13, resulting in a long-term pattern of alcohol abuse until she achieved sobriety at age 44. Sally expressed that she never felt that her mother would care and thus never disclosed the abuse as a child. When she finally did disclose her sexual abuse history when she was in her 30's, her mother responded indifferently, stating, "I knew I threw you to the wolves, I didn't know they were that hungry."

In this case example, Sally experienced supervision, physical, and emotional neglect. The lack of love she perceived from her mother may be hypothesized as a reason why she feels innately unworthy and unlovable. Her history of childhood neglect and attachment insecurity to her mother resulted in her seeking love and acceptance outside of the home, increasing her risk for revictimization (i.e., sexual abuse) (Gold, 2000; Ney et al. 1994). The childhood sexual abuse she endured was a result of a lack of supervision and inadequate skills for assessing trustworthiness, contributing to an inability to differentiate between trustworthy and untrustworthy individuals, as well as how to ask for help. These early childhood experiences of neglect and sexual abuse influenced her subsequent alcoholism to "numb" the pain and instead led to decades of detachment, fear, and depression.

Within CTT, treatment goals include the following: (1) building a collaborative therapeutic relationship; (2) client-guided conceptualization to facilitate exploration of the impact of family environment and traumatic experiences on present day beliefs and functioning; and (3) developing adaptive skills for daily living (Gold, 2000). Throughout her treatment, it was evident that Sally was motivated; however, she admitted having difficulty trusting others and "letting people in." The importance of being wary of the therapist initially was emphasized and she was encouraged to listen to what this clinician said, watch what she did, and decide, in time, if she was consistent and trustworthy. Fostering a safe, non-judgmental space was paramount in making sure Sally felt comfortable in exploring her current difficulties, her upbringing, and her trauma with this clinician in future sessions. Special attention was given to exploring the inherent power differential in the therapy relationship and how to minimize this differential as this was of concern to her because of her trauma history. The collaborative nature of our working relationship empowered Sally to be assertive, instilled a sense of control over the trajectory of treatment, and provided Sally with validation and a corrective interpersonal relationship.

In regard to client guided conceptualization, Sally focused primarily on her desire to understand her dissociative and depressive symptoms, primarily her view of herself as "incompetent and unsuccessful" at work, "unworthy of love," and estranged from others. Perhaps most significant, for Sally, was her inability to "appropriately" express emotions and connect with her feelings. During this stage, Sally explored her conceptualization of how these symptoms came to be and how they were maintained throughout her life through various experiences in various contexts. It was paramount that Sally was undeniably the expert of her experience and her symptoms; this approach allowed for her to make more meaningful and true connections and hypotheses about the causes of her problems and fostered a sense of mastery over her experience. During this phase, Sally began to explore why she felt guarded and mistrustful of others. Similarly, she began to question how her abuse impacted her current functioning and suspected that her upbringing and her trauma contributed to her persistent belief that she was "unlovable." Client guided conceptualization also helped strengthen the collaborative relationship in that it was an explicit way in which Sally was actively collaborating in treatment and coming to her own conclusions about her experiences.

In regard to therapist guided skills transmission, Sally was taught to identify her triggers for dissociative symptoms (e.g., stress, anticipating negative affect, insecurity, and trauma memories) and to counter dissociation using core mindfulness skills, which consists of observing, describing, participating in her present sensory experience. Additionally, emotion regulation skills were taught including naming and understanding the purpose of emotions, factors that make it difficult to regulate emotions, and Linehan's (2015) model of describing emotion. CTT with Sally facilitated her improved interpersonal relationships with family and friends, allowed her to process her trauma and neglect, and build a healthy relationship with her elderly mother.

Childhood Neglect and Attachment Insecurity

"Maria," a 36-year-old Hispanic woman, presented for treatment with symptoms of depression and depersonalization. She reported that she felt "empty inside" and did not feel "connected to anyone or anything." Maria explained that she felt detached from her own emotions and found it hard to connect with people, whether they be co-workers, friends, or family members. She stated this was particularly problematic as she could not "connect" with her four-year-old son because she felt like she "was in another world, so far away from everyone." She stated that all her friendships were "surface level" and "shallow." She reported a strained relationship with her parents and siblings, stating they "only reach out to [her] when they need something."

Maria described her childhood as "chaotic and unpredictable." She said that she "had to hustle and take care of [herself] because no one ever looked out for [her]." She indicated that this included stealing food for her family and selling drugs to buy new clothes. She explained that her mother moved her and her younger siblings from the Caribbean to Florida so that they could become legal citizens. However, her mother had to return to the Caribbean and consequently left Maria and her siblings in the care of her grandparents. Maria reported that she had to take care of her siblings and took on the role of a parentified child. In addition to the stress of acculturation, caring for young siblings, and adolescence, Maria also endured molestation by a family member. Maria expressed that she never felt close to anyone after the molestation began and stated that she had "trust issues." When Maria's mother and father moved to Florida permanently, Maria disclosed her sexual abuse history and she stated that her parents "swept it under the rug." She indicated that she found it "impossible to feel love" for her family and stated that she has always had difficulty attaching to others, keeping her distance "in fear of being hurt again."

Using Bronfenbrenner's Ecological Model (1979) to conceptualize Maria, it is evident that the environmental context in which she grew up negatively impacted her development emotionally and psychologically. Maria's microsystem consisted of her parents who were neglectful and abused substances and her siblings who were dependent on her. She rarely had time for friends at school and often found the classroom to be an invalidating environment because she struggled to learn English and was often called stupid. The interaction between these microsystems was lacking; Maria's parents were neglectful of Maria and her siblings and Maria had to take on a parenting role at a young age. Additionally, they did not engage with her teachers and were not aware of Maria's difficulties at school. Maria's exosystem consisted of her grandparents, her parent's immigrant status, and the impoverished neighborhood in which she grew up. These systems added stress and "chaos" to Maria's development as her grandfather molested her and her grandmother "covered it up." She reported being in constant fear that her parents would be deported and never felt as though she could feel attached to anyone because they could leave her at any time. This relates to the microsystem in which she was reared as well – laws related to deportation, Hispanic culture vs. Caucasian American culture, and the economic system. Although Maria was able to distance herself from her family and was able to continue through school and obtain her Masters, her development of attachment security remained stunted. The lack of parental warmth, affection, or supervision facilitated her view of herself as isolated and detached. Growing up, the only person she could rely on was herself.

Treatment focused on fostering attachment security with her son, husband, and friends. Special attention was given to her role as a mother as she wanted to "avoid making the same mistakes [her] parents did." Core mindfulness skills were utilized to help keep Maria present in the moment when interacting with others, observing and participating in the moment. Emotion regulation skills were utilized to help Maria identify, connect with, and express her emotions appropriately. When treatment was completed, Maria was confident in her ability to be a "good mother" to her son and reported feeling "joy" and "connected" to him and her husband. She reported finding interpersonal interactions "easier" and less "overwhelming" because she could now "relate to other people." Maria was also acutely aware of how the environment around her and the people she associates with impact her development and her son's development. She was committed to surrounding herself and her son with positive influences and being more involved in her son's schooling and friend groups.

Chapter 7
Unveiling Covert Abuse

Neglect has been found to adversely influence neurological development, attachment formation, and both child and adult psychopathology. Due to the covert nature of neglect, detection of neglectful parenting may be difficult to determine by both uninformed and informed providers; this may be exceptionally challenging when faced with subtypes of neglect where physical harm is less apparent. Difficulties in establishing a clear definition of neglect have implications for both the research and legal contexts (i.e., incidents of neglect resulting in a referral to child protective services agencies). As a result, it is important to be abreast of associated contextual risk factors, including parental substance abuse or mental health stressors, low SES, and young maternal age, among others. Similarly, problem child behaviors, deficient physical development (i.e., associated with malnutrition), impaired intellectual functioning, and limited peer support may serve as red flags that the child is being reared in an impoverished or neglectful family environment. Consequently, primary care physicians are in a unique evaluative position of monitoring a child's health and development, and may be able to provide resources to families where neglect is suspected. Teachers may also have the ability to recognize when a child is exhibiting "symptoms" of neglect, such as an inability to grasp grade-appropriate information, coupled with behavioral difficulties, malnourishment, or inappropriate or dirty clothing.

Early prevention and intervention is key, and often includes both the parent(s) and child. Home visiting programs have demonstrated success in improving the quality of at-home parenting in families deemed at risk for, or having been identified as, being neglectful. Parent education programs have also been emphasized in the literature, as these programs facilitate more appropriate parent-child interactions and a more thorough understanding of child development and the ways in which ineffective parenting influences such development. For children, therapy and peer support, and sometimes being removed from the impoverished environment, if in early childhood, have been demonstrated to contribute to improvements in behavioral, social, and cognitive functioning. In adulthood, this therapy may be focused on skills acquisition in an effort to remediate gaps and warps in development associated with a lack of skills transmission from the parents. Regardless, clinical attention should consider the presence of childhood neglect in therapy and assess its implications when informing treatment in both children and adults.

In conclusion, neglect is not only a problem within a family; rather it is a social problem. Without facilitation from extrafamilial individuals within the community with access to at-risk children, prevention and intervention efforts may not be possible or effective. Our failure as a community to prevent and intervene leaves neglected children at risk for myriad problems in adjustment and functioning. However, if detected, those problems have the potential to be remediated, and the children experiencing them have the potential to thrive.

Future Directions

More research is required to examine neglect independently of co-occurring maltreatment to obtain a comprehensive understanding of its implications for both child and adult functioning. However, due to the frequency at which various forms of neglect and child maltreatment co-occur, the existing body of research may, in fact, be relevant and generalizable to survivors of childhood neglect, abuse, and maltreatment. Future research may further explore the independent implications of different subtypes of neglect (e.g., physical, emotional, medical, supervisory), associated risk and protective factors, and intervention strategies.

The existing body of research may benefit from additional prospective and longitudinal studies. Prospective studies utilizing documented cases of childhood neglect, where other types of childhood abuse (e.g., physical, sexual) are not found may serve to provide a comparison group for those children exposed to multiple forms of maltreatment, allowing for increased clarity into the unique long-term effects of childhood neglect on biopsychosocial development across the lifespan. In addition to the use of self-report questionnaires, the use of neuropsychological and neuroimaging assessments provide increased clarity regarding the cognitive and neurological deficits in adult survivors of childhood neglect. A more thorough understanding of the various biopsychosocial implications of childhood neglect will serve to better guide future interventions and treatment, providing more comprehensive resources to those affected by a lack of childhood care.

References

Ainsworth, M. D. S., & Bell, S. M. (1970). Attachment, exploration, and separation: Illustrated by the behavior of one-year-olds in a strange situation. *Child Development, 41*, 49–67. https://doi.org/10.2307/1127388

Ainsworth, M. D. S., & Wittig, B. A. (1969). Attachment and exploratory behavior of one-year-olds in a strange situation. In B. M. Foss (Ed.), *Determinants of infant behavior* (Vol. 4, pp. 111–136). London: Methuen.

Alexander, P. C. (2009). Childhood trauma, attachment, and abuse by multiple partners. *Psychological Trauma: Theory, Research, Practice, and Policy, 1*, 78–88. https://doi.org/10.1037/a0015254

Allen, R. E., & Oliver, J. M. (1982). The effects of child maltreatment on language development. *Child Abuse & Neglect, 6*, 299–305. https://doi.org/10.1016/0145-2134(82)90033-3

Allin, H., Wathen, C. N., & MacMillan, H. (2005). Treatment of child neglect: A systematic review. *Canadian Journal of Psychiatry, 50*, 497–504. https://doi.org/10.1177/070674370505000810

American Psychiatric Association. (2013). *Diagnostic and statistical manual of mental disorders-5* (5th ed.). Washington, DC: American Psychiatric Association.

Barth, R. P. (2009). Preventing child abuse and neglect with parent training: Evidence and opportunities. *The Future of Children, 19*, 95–118. https://doi.org/10.1353/foc.0.0031

Bifulco, A., Kwon, J., Jacobs, C., Moran, P. M., Bunn, A., & Beer, N. (2006). Adult attachment style as mediator between childhood neglect/abuse and adult depression and anxiety. *Social Psychiatry and Psychiatric Epidemiology, 41*, 796–805. https://doi.org/10.1007/s00127-006-0101-z

Bogdan, R., Williamson, D. E., & Hariri, A. R. (2012). Mineralocorticoid receptor Iso/Val (rs5522) genotype moderates the association between previous childhood emotional neglect and amygdala reactivity. *American Journal of Psychiatry, 169*, 515–522. https://doi.org/10.1176/appi.ajp.2011.11060855

Borelli, J. L., Compare, A., Snavely, J. E., & Decio, V. (2015). Reflective functioning moderates the association between perceptions of parental neglect and attachment in adolescence. *Psychoanalytic Psychology, 32*, 23–35. https://doi.org/10.1037/a0037858

Bowlby, J. (1969). *Attachment and loss*. New York: Basic Books.

Boyd, R. C., Zayas, L. H., & McKee, M. D. (2006). Mother-infant interaction, life events and prenatal and postpartum depressive symptoms among urban minority women in primary care. *Maternal and Child Health Journal, 10*, 139–148. https://doi.org/10.1007/s10995-005-0042-2

Bretherton, I. (1992). The origins of attachment theory: John Bowlby and Mary Ainsworth. *Developmental Psychology, 28*, 759. https://doi.org/10.1037/0012-1649.28.5.759

Bronfenbrenner, U. (1979). *The ecology of human development: Experiments by nature and design*. Cambridge, MA: Harvard University Press.

Brown, J., Cohen, P., Johnson, J. G., & Salzinger, S. (1998). A longitudinal analysis of risk factors for child maltreatment: Findings of a 17-year prospective study of officially recorded and self-reported child abuse and neglect. *Child Abuse and Neglect, 22*, 1065–1078. https://doi.org/10.1016/S0145-2134(98)00087-8

Caldwell, R. A., Bogat, G. A., & Davidson II, W. S. (1988). The assessment of child abuse potential and the prevention of child abuse and neglect: A policy analysis. *American Journal of Community Psychology, 16*, 609–624. https://doi.org/10.1007/BF00930017

Cancel, A., Comte, M., Truillet, R., Boukezzi, S., Rousseau, P. F., Zendjidjian, X. Y., et al. (2015). Childhood neglect predicts disorganization in schizophrenia through grey matter decrease in dorsolateral prefrontal cortex. *Acta Psychiatrica Scandinavica, 132*, 244–256. https://doi.org/10.1111/acps.12455

Carlson, N. R. (2013). *Physiology of behavior: Pearson new international edition*. Harlow, UK: Pearson Higher Education.

Chapple, C. L., Tyler, K. A., & Bersani, B. E. (2005). Child neglect and adolescent violence: Examining the effects of self-control and peer rejection. *Violence and Victims, 20*, 39–53. https://doi.org/10.1891/0886-6708.2005.20.1.39

Chaudron, L. H. (2003). Postpartum depression: What pediatricians need to know? *Pediatrics, 24*, 154–161. https://doi.org/10.1542/pir.24-5-154

Claussen, A. H., & Crittenden, P. M. (1991). Physical and psychological maltreatment: Relations among types of maltreatment. *Child Abuse & Neglect, 15*, 5–18. https://doi.org/10.1016/0145-2134(91)90085-R

Collins, N. L., & Allard, L. M. (2001). Cognitive representations of attachment: The content and function of working models. *Blackwell Handbook of Social Psychology: Interpersonal Processes, 2*, 60–85. https://doi.org/10.1002/9780470998557.ch3

Cowen, P. S. (1999). Child neglect: Injuries of omission. *Pediatric Nursing, 25*, 401–418. Retrieved from HighBeam Research: https://www.highbeam.com/doc/1G1-55577822.html

Crockett, L. J., & Randall, B. A. (2006). Linking adolescent family and peer relationships to the quality of young adult romantic relationships: The mediating role of conflict tactics. *Journal of Social and Personal Relationships, 23*, 761–780. https://doi.org/10.1177/0265407506068262

De Bellis, M. D. (2005). The psychobiology of neglect. *Child Maltreatment, 10*, 150–172. https://doi.org/10.1177/1077559505275116

De Bellis, M. D., Hooper, S. R., Spratt, E. G., & Woolley, D. P. (2009). Neuropsychological findings in childhood neglect and their relationships to pediatric PTSD. *Journal of the International Neuropsychological Society, 15*, 868–878. https://doi.org/10.1017/S1355617709990464

Dean, A. L., Malik, M. M., Richards, W., & Stringer, S. A. (1986). Effects of parental maltreatment on children's conceptions of interpersonal relationships. *Developmental Psychology, 22*, 617–626. https://doi.org/10.1037/0012-1649.22.5.617

Dishion, T. J., Mun, C. J., Drake, E. C., Tein, J. Y., Shaw, D. S., & Wilson, M. (2015). A transactional approach to preventing early childhood neglect: The family check-up as a public health strategy. *Development and Psychopathology, 27*, 1647–1660. https://doi.org/10.1017/S0954579415001005

Dubowitz, H. (1994). Neglecting the neglect of neglect. *Journal of Interpersonal Violence, 9*, 556–560. https://doi.org/10.1177/088626094009004010

Enoch, M. A. (2011). The role of early life stress as a predictor for alcohol and drug dependence. *Psychopharmacology, 214*, 17–31. https://doi.org/10.1007/s00213-010-1916-6

Erickson, M. F., Egeland, B., & Pianta, R. (1989). The effects of maltreatment on the development of young children. In D. Cicchetti & V. Carlson (Eds.), *Child maltreatment* (pp. 647–684). Cambridge, UK: Cambridge University Press.

Evans, R., Garner, P., & Honig, A. S. (2014). Prevention of violence, abuse and neglect in early childhood: A review of the literature on research, policy and practice. *Early Child Development and Care, 184*, 1295–1335. https://doi.org/10.1080/03004430.2014.91032

Fahy, A. E., Stansfeld, S. A., Smuk, M., Lain, D., van der Horst, M., Vickerstaff, S., & Clark, C. (2017). Longitudinal associations of experiences of adversity and socioeconomic disadvantage during childhood with labour force participation and exit in later adulthood. *Social Science & Medicine, 183*, 80–87. https://doi.org/10.1016/j.socscimed.2017.04.023

References

Felitti, V. J., Anda, R. F., Nordenberg, D., Williamson, D. F., Spitz, A. M., Edwards, V., et al. (1998). Relationship of childhood abuse and household dysfunction to many of the leading causes of death in adults: The adverse childhood experiences (ACE) study. *American Journal of Preventive Medicine, 14*, 245–258. https://doi.org/10.1016/S0749-3797(98)00017-8

Florida Abuse Hotline. (2013). *Reporting abuse of children and vulnerable adults*. Tallahassee, FL.: Retrieved from https://www.dcf.state.fl.us/programs/abuse/publications/mandatedreporters.pdf

Frodi, A., & Smetana, J. (1984). Abused, neglected, and nonmaltreated preschoolers' ability to discriminate emotions in others: The effects of IQ. *Child Abuse & Neglect, 8*, 459–465. https://doi.org/10.1016/0145-2134(84)90027-9

Gauthier, L., Stollak, G., Messé, L., & Aronoff, J. (1996). Recall of childhood neglect and physical abuse as differential predictors of current psychological functioning. *Child Abuse & Neglect, 20*, 549–559. https://doi.org/10.1016/0145-2134(96)00043-9

Gerra, G., Somaini, L., Manfredini, M., Raggi, M. A., Saracino, M. A., Amore, M., et al. (2014). Dysregulated responses to emotions among abstinent heroin users: Correlation with childhood neglect and addiction severity. *Progress in Neuro-Psychopharmacology and Biological Psychiatry, 48*, 220–228. https://doi.org/10.1016/j.pnpbp.2013.10.011

Glaser, D. (2000). Child abuse and neglect and the brain—A review. *Journal of Child Psychology and Psychiatry, 41*, 97–116. https://doi.org/10.1017/S0021963099004990

Gold, S. N. (2000). *Not trauma alone: Therapy for child abuse survivors in family and social context*. Philadelphia: Routledge.

Gold, S. N., Hyman, S. M., & Andres-Hyman, R. C. (2004). Family of origin environments in two clinical samples of survivors of intra-familial, extra-familial, and both types of sexual abuse. *Child Abuse & Neglect, 28*, 1199–1212. https://doi.org/10.1016/j.chiabu.2004.07.001

Grace, S. L., Evindar, A., & Stewart, D. E. (2003). The effect of postpartum depression on child cognitive development and behavior: A review and critical analysis of the literature. *Archives of Women's Mental Health, 6*, 263–274. https://doi.org/10.1007/s00737-003-0024-6

Grassi-Oliveira, R., & Stein, L. M. (2008). Childhood maltreatment associated with PTSD and emotional distress in low-income adults: The burden of neglect. *Child Abuse & Neglect, 32*, 1089–1094. https://doi.org/10.1016/j.chiabu.2008.05.008

Grossman, F. K., Spinazzola, J., Zucker, M., & Hopper, E. (2017). Treating adult survivors of childhood emotional abuse and neglect: A new framework. *American Journal of Orthopsychiatriy, 87*, 86–93. https://doi.org/10.1037/ort0000225

Guterman, N. B. (1997). Early prevention of physical child abuse and neglect: Existing evidence and future directions. *Child Maltreatment, 2*, 12–34. https://doi.org/10.1177/1077559597002001003

Haga, S. M., Ulleberg, P., Slinning, K., Kraft, P., Steen, T. B., & Staff, A. (2012). A longitudinal study of postpartum depressive symptoms: Multilevel growth curve analyses of emotion regulation strategies, breastfeeding self-efficacy, and social support. *Archives of Women's Mental Health, 15*, 175–184. https://doi.org/10.1007/s00737-012-0274-2

Hart, S., Field, T., del Valle, C., & Pelaez-Nogueras, M. (1998). Depressed mothers' interactions with their one-year-old infants. *Infant Behavior & Development, 21*, 519–525. https://doi.org/10.1016/S0163-6383(98)90024-8

Hartley, C. C. (2002). The co-occurrence of child maltreatment and domestic violence: Examining both neglect and child physical abuse. *Child Maltreatment, 7*, 349–358. https://doi.org/10.1177/107755902237264

Hazan, C., & Shaver, P. R. (1987). Romantic love conceptualized as an attachment process. *Journal of Personality and Social Psychology, 52*, 511–524. https://doi.org/10.1037/0022-3514.52.3.511

Herman, J. (1997). *Trauma and recovery: The aftermath of violence – from domestic abuse to political terror*. New York: Basic Books.

Hildyard, K. L., & Wolfe, D. A. (2002). Child neglect: Developmental issues and outcomes. *Child Abuse & Neglect, 26*, 679–695. https://doi.org/10.1016/S0145-2134(02)00341-1

Hobbs, C. J., & Wynne, J. M. (2002). Neglect of neglect. *Current Pediatrics, 22*, 144–150. https://doi.org/10.1054/cupe.2001.0266

Howard, K. S., & Brooks-Gunn, J. (2009). The role of home-visiting programs in preventing child abuse and neglect. *The Future of Children, 19,* 119–146. https://doi.org/10.1353/foc.0.0032

Johnson, J. J., Smailes, E. M., Cohen, P., Brown, J., & Bernstein, D. P. (2000). Associations between four types of childhood neglect and personality disorder symptoms during adolescence and early adulthood: Findings of a community-based longitudinal study. *Journal of Personality Disorders, 14,* 171–187. https://doi.org/10.1521/pedi.2000.14.2.171

Joseph, R. (1999). Environmental influences on neural plasticity, the limbic system, emotional development and attachment: A review. *Child Psychiatry and Human Development, 29,* 189–208. https://doi.org/10.1023/A:1022660923605

Kaplan, S. J., Pelcovitz, D., & Labruna, V. (1999). Child and adolescent abuse and neglect research: A review of the past 10 years. Part I: Physical and emotional abuse and neglect. *Journal of the American Academy of Child & Adolescent Psychiatry, 38,* 1214–1222.

Kessler, R. C., McLaughlin, K. A., Green, J. G., Gruber, M. J., Sampson, N. A., Zaslavsky, A. M., et al. (2010). Childhood adversities and adult psychopathology in the WHO World mental health surveys. *The British Journal of Psychiatry, 197,* 378–385. https://doi.org/10.1192/bjp.bp.110.080499

Kim, J., & Cicchetti, D. (2010). Longitudinal pathways linking child maltreatment, emotion regulation, peer relations, and psychopathology. *Journal of Child Psychology and Psychiatry, 51,* 706–716. https://doi.org/10.1111/j.1469-7610.2009.02202.x

Lawson, G. M., Camins, J. S., Wisse, L., Wu, J., Duda, J. T., Cook, P. A., et al. (2017). Childhood socioeconomic status and childhood maltreatment: Distinct associations with brain structure. *PLoS One, 12,* 1–16. https://doi.org/10.6084/m9.figshare.4811404

Levy, K. N., Ellison, W. D., Scott, L. N., & Bernecker, S. L. (2011). Attachment style. *Journal of Clinical Psychology, 67,* 193–203. https://doi.org/10.1002/jclp.20756

Linehan, M. M. (2015). *DBT® skills training manual* (2nd ed.). New York: Guilford Publications.

Maheu, F. S., Dozier, M., Guyer, A. E., Mandell, D., Peloso, E., Poeth, K., et al. (2010). A preliminary study of medial temporal lobe function in youths with a history of caregiver deprivation and emotional neglect. *Cognitive, Affective, & Behavioral Neuroscience, 10,* 34–49. https://doi.org/10.3758/CABN.10.1.34

Maleck, S., & Papp, L. M. (2015). Childhood risky family environments and romantic relationship functioning among young adult dating couples. *Journal of Family Issues, 36,* 567. https://doi.org/10.1177/0192513X13491749

McDaniel, B., & Dillenburger, K. (2007). Can childhood neglect be assessed and prevented through childcare skills training? *Child Abuse Review, 16,* 120–129. https://doi.org/10.1002/car.950

Mikton, C., & Butchart, A. (2009). Child maltreatment prevention: A systematic review of reviews. *Bulletin of the World Health Organization, 87,* 353–361. https://doi.org/10.2471/BLT.08.057075

Milner, J. (1994). Assessing physical child abuse risk: The child abuse potential inventory. *Clinical Psychology Review, 14,* 547–583. https://doi.org/10.1016/0272-7358(94)90017-5

Moxley, K. M., Squires, J., & Lindstrom, L. (2012). Early intervention and maltreated children: A current look at the child abuse prevention and treatment act and part C. *Infants & Young Children, 25,* 3–18. https://doi.org/10.1097/IYC.0b013e3182392ff0

Murray, L. (1992). The impact of postnatal depression on infant development. *Journal of Child Psychology and Psychiatry, 33,* 543–561. https://doi.org/10.1111/j.1469-7610.1992.tb00890.x

Murray, L., & Cooper, P. J. (1996). The impact of postpartum depression on child development. *International Review of Psychiatry, 8,* 55–63. https://doi.org/10.3109/09540269609037817

Ney, P. G., Fung, T., & Wickett, A. R. (1994). The worst combinations of child abuse and neglect. *Child Abuse & Neglect, 18,* 705–714. https://doi.org/10.1016/0145-2134(94)00037-9

Nikulina, V., & Widom, C. S. (2014). Do race, neglect, and childhood poverty predict physical health in adulthood? A multilevel prospective analysis. *Child Abuse & Neglect, 28,* 414–424. https://doi.org/10.1016/j.chiabu.2013.09.007

Olds, D. L., Eckenrode, J., Henderson, C. R., Kitzman, H., Powers, J., Cole, R., et al. (1997). Long-term effects of home visitation on maternal life course and child abuse and neglect:

References

Fifteen-year follow-up of a randomized trial. *Journal of the American Medical Association, 278*, 637–643. https://doi.org/10.1001/jama.1997.03550080047038

Pace, C. S., & Zavattini, G. C. (2011). 'Adoption and attachment theory' the attachment models of adoptive mothers and the revision of attachment patterns of their late-adopted children. *Child: Care, Health and Development, 37*, 82–88. https://doi.org/10.1111/j.1365-2214.2010.01135.x

Paris, J. (2013). *The intelligent clinician's guide to the DSM-5*. New York: Oxford University Press.

Pechtel, P., & Pizzagalli, D. A. (2011). Effects of early life stress on cognitive and affective function: An integrated review of human literature. *Psychopharmacology, 214*, 55–70. https://doi.org/10.1007/s00213-010-2009-2

Perry, B. D. (2002). Childhood experience and the expression of genetic potential: What childhood neglect tells us about nature and nurture. *Brain and Mind, 3*, 79–100. https://doi.org/10.1023/A:1016557824657

Pignatelli, A. M., Wampers, M., Loriedo, C., Biondi, M., & Vanderlinden, J. (2016). Childhood neglect in eating disorders: A systematic review and meta-analysis. *Journal of Trauma & Dissociation, 18*, 100–115. https://doi.org/10.1080/15299732.2016.1198951

Powers, A., Ressler, K. J., & Bradley, R. G. (2009). The protective role of friendship on the effects of childhood abuse and depression. *Depression and Anxiety, 26*, 46–53. https://doi.org/10.1002/da.20534

Roisman, G. I., Collins, A. W., Sroufe, A. L., & Egeland, B. (2005). Predictors of young adults' representations of and behavior in their current romantic relationship: Prospective tests of the prototype hypothesis. *Attachment & Human Development, 7*, 102–121. https://doi.org/10.1080/14616730500134928

Sedlak, A., & Broadhurst, D. (1996). *The third national incidence study on child abuse and neglect (NIS-3)*. Washington, DC: U.S. Department of Health and Human Services.

Shin, S. H., Miller, D. P., & Teicher, M. H. (2013). Exposure to childhood neglect and physical abuse and developmental trajectories of heavy episodic drinking from early adolescence into young adulthood. *Drug and Alcohol Dependence, 127*, 31–38. https://doi.org/10.1016/j.drugalcdep.2012.06.005

Shipman, K., Edwards, A., Brown, A., Swisher, L., & Jennings, E. (2005). Managing emotion in a maltreating context: A pilot study examining child neglect. *Child Abuse & Neglect, 29*, 1015–1029. https://doi.org/10.1016/j.chiabu.2005.01.006

Slack, K. S., Holl, J. L., McDaniel, M., Yoo, J., & Bolger, K. (2004). Understanding the risks of child neglect: An exploration of poverty and parenting characteristics. *Child Maltreatment, 9*, 395–408. https://doi.org/10.1177/1077559504269193

Sperry, D. M., & Widom, C. S. (2013). Child abuse and neglect, social support, and psychopathology in adulthood: A prospective investigation. *Child Abuse & Neglect, 37*, 415–425. https://doi.org/10.1016/j.chiabu.2013.02.006

Spertus, I. L., Yehuda, R., Wong, C. M., Halligan, S., & Seremetis, S. V. (2003). Childhood emotional abuse and neglect as predictors of psychological and physical symptoms in women presenting to a primary care practice. *Child Abuse & Neglect, 27*, 1247–1258. https://doi.org/10.1016/j.chiabu.2003.05.001

Sroufe, L. A. (1988). The role of infant-caregiver attachment in development. In J. Belsky & T. Nezworski (Eds.), *Clinical implications of attachment* (pp. 18–38). Hillsdale, NJ: Lawrence Erlbaum Associates, Inc., Publishers.

Stein, A., Gath, D. H., Bucher, J., Bond, A., Day, A., & Cooper, P. J. (1991). The relationship between post-natal depression and mother-child interaction. *The British Journal of Psychiatry, 158*, 46–52. https://doi.org/10.1192/bjp.158.1.46

Stern, D. N. (1985). *The interpersonal world of the infant*. New York: Basic Books.

Stirling, J., & Amaya-Jackson, L. (2008). Understanding the behavioral and emotional consequences of child abuse. *Pediatrics, 122*, 667–673. https://doi.org/10.1542/peds.2008-1885

Strathearn, L., Gray, P. H., O'Callaghan, M. J., & Wood, D. O. (2001). Childhood neglect and cognitive development in extremely low birth weight infants: A prospective study. *Pediatrics, 108*, 142–151. https://doi.org/10.1542/peds.108.1.142

Straus, M. A., & Kantor, G. K. (2005). Definition and measurement of neglectful behavior: Some principles and guidelines. *Child Abuse & Neglect, 29*, 19–29. https://doi.org/10.1016/j.chiabu.2004.08.005

Straus, M. A., Kinard, E. M., & Williams, L. M. (1995). *The neglect scale.* Durham, NH: Manuscript, University of New Hampshire, Family Research Laboratory.

Tanner, K. & Turney, D. (2003). What do we know about child neglect? A critical review of the literature and its application to social work practice. *Child and Family Social Work, 8*, 25–34

Teicher, M. H., Dumont, N. L., Ito, Y., Vaituzis, C., Giedd, J. N., & Andersen, S. L. (2004). Childhood neglect is associated with reduced corpus callosum area. *Biological Psychiatry, 56*, 80–85. https://doi.org/10.1016/j.biopsych.2004.03.016

U.S. Department of Health and Human Services, Administration for Children and Families, Administration on Children, Youth and Families, Children's Bureau (2013) Child maltreatment 2012. Retrived from http://www.acf.hhs.gov/programs/cb/research-data-technology/statistics-research/child-maltreatment

Underwood, M. K., & Rosen, L. H. (2009). Gender, peer relations, and challenges for girlfriends and boyfriends coming together in adolescence. *Psychology of Women Quarterly, 33*, 16–20. https://doi.org/10.1111/j.1471-6402.2008.01468.x

Walker, E. A., Gelfand, A., Katon, W. J., Koss, M. P., Von Korff, M., Bernstein, D., & Russo, J. (1999). Adult health status of women with histories of childhood abuse and neglect. *The American Journal of Medicine, 107*, 332–339. https://doi.org/10.1016/S0002-9343(99)00235-1

Wark, M. J., Kruczek, T., & Boley, A. (2003). Emotional neglect and family structure: Impact on student functioning. *Child Abuse & Neglect, 27*, 1033–1043. https://doi.org/10.1016/S0145-2134(03)00162-5

Watts-English, T., Fortson, B. L., Gibler, N., Hooper, S. R., & De Bellis, M. D. (2006). The psychobiology of maltreatment in childhood. *Journal of Social Issues, 62*, 717–736. https://doi.org/10.1111/j.1540-4560.2006.00484.x

Weigel, D. J. (2007). Parental divorce and the types of commitment-related messages people gain from their families of origin. *Journal of Divorce & Remarriage, 47*, 15–32. https://doi.org/10.1300/J087v47n01_02

Wekerle, C., & Wolfe, D. A. (1993). Prevention of child physical abuse and neglect: Promising new directions. *Clinical Psychology Review, 13*, 501–540. https://doi.org/10.1016/0272-7358(93)90044-M

Wells, K. M. (2006). Substance abuse and child maltreatment. In C. R. Brittain (Ed.), *Understanding the medical diagnosis of child maltreatment: A guide for nonmedical professionals* (3rd ed., pp. 179–189). New York: Oxford University Press.

Widom, C. S. (2000). Childhood victimization: Early adversity, later psychopathology. *National Institute of Justice Journal, 242*, 3–9. Retrieved from https://www.ncjrs.gov/pdffiles1/jr000242b.pdf

Widom, C. S., Czaja, S., Wilson, H. W., Allwood, M., & Chauhan, P. (2012). Do the long-tern consequences of neglect differ for children of difference races and ethnic backgrounds? *Child Maltreatment, 18*, 42–55. https://doi.org/10.1177/1077559512460728.

Widom, C. S., Czaja, S., Wilson, H. W., Allwood, M., & Chauhan, P. (2013). Do the long-term consequences of neglect differ for children of different races and ethnic backgrounds? *Child Maltreatment, 18*, 42–55. https://doi.org/10.1177/1077559512460728

Wolfe, D. A., & Wekerle, C. (1993). Treatment strategies for child physical abuse and neglect: A critical progress report. *Clinical Psychology Review, 13*, 473–500. https://doi.org/10.1016/0272-7358(93)90043-L

Young, J. C., & Widom, C. S. (2014). Long-term effects of child abuse and neglect on emotion processing in adulthood. *Child Abuse & Neglect, 38*, 1369–1381. https://doi.org/10.1016/j.chiabu.2014.03.008

Printed in the United States
By Bookmasters